LITERACY

LITERACY
A Way Out for At-Risk Youth

Jennifer Sweeney

LIBRARIES UNLIMITED

AN IMPRINT OF ABC-CLIO, LLC
Santa Barbara, California • Denver, Colorado • Oxford, England

Library of Congress Cataloging-in-Publication Data

Sweeney, Jennifer.
  Literacy : a way out for at-risk youth / Jennifer Sweeney.
    pages cm
  Includes bibliographical references and index.
    ISBN 978–1–59884–674–4 (pbk.) — ISBN 978–1–59884–675–1 (ebook) (print) 1. Libraries and juvenile delinquents—United States. 2. Prison libraries—United States. 3. Libraries and prisons—United States. 4. Juvenile corrections—United States. 5. Literacy—Social aspects—United States. 6. Literacy programs—United States. 7. Problem youth—Books and reading—United States. 8. Juvenile delinquents—Books and reading—United States. 9. Juvenile delinquents—Education—United States. 10. Juvenile delinquents—Rehabilitation—United States. I. Title
  Z711.92.J88S94 2012
  027.62′6—dc23   2011042804

ISBN: 978–1–59884–674–4
EISBN: 978–1–59884–675–1

16 15 14 13 12   1 2 3 4 5

This book is also available on the World Wide Web as an eBook.
Visit www.abc-clio.com for details.

Libraries Unlimited
An Imprint of ABC-CLIO, LLC

ABC-CLIO, LLC
130 Cremona Drive, P.O. Box 1911
Santa Barbara, California 93116-1911

This book is printed on acid-free paper ∞

Manufactured in the United States of America

To all the folks out there getting the books to the kids.

Contents

Illustrations

Preface

My purpose in this book was to discern those aspects of juvenile detention librarianship that set it apart from other young adult collections and services, as well as from libraries in adult correctional institutions and jails. Library service to juvenile offenders is a truly unique and remarkable branch of library work. I have to admit that when I started this project, I thought I would simply take what we knew already on developing and running adult prison libraries and modify that to work with juvenile services. I was wrong.

What I found was that library service to this population of underserved teens has its own poignant and moving history that should stir even the most jaded information professional among us. What is more, I discovered that it is one of the few services today that remains in a stage of "pioneering, innovation, and enthusiasm" as Sara Innis Fenwick would have said. That is not to say that the information technology unfolding all around us every day does not keep us in a constant state of excitement, but library service to juveniles in detention is itself still in its infancy, despite the fact that we have been honing young adult library services for over 100 years, and prison library services for twice that long.

Education, for example, was not mandated in juvenile detention until the mid-1970s. Think about that.

In this book I have attempted to share the stories of two dozen JDC librarians who had the patience to talk with me, someone who knew absolutely nothing about prison librarianship or juvenile delinquency (and almost that much about youth services), and explain what they do and why they do it. Their perspectives, impressions, wisdom, and advice provide the central themes for this work.

In no way does this book purport to tell how it is everywhere, in every detention center library. We do not, in fact, know much about the actual extent of library services in this area: to date, there has been no comprehensive survey of library services to juveniles in detention.[1] This book is merely an exploration of what some libraries in detention look like, and a description of what some of the pioneering librarians in this field are doing right now. This book is also not a how-to book. Although there are some real gems of advice for the newcomer to the field scattered throughout, this book does not provide comprehensive hands-on techniques for operating a juvenile detention center (JDC) library on the ground. If you want to learn how to build and run a good library for young people, there are many excellent resources out there already. I recommend *Connecting Young Adults and Libraries* by Jones, Gorman, and Suellentrop for great advice and programming ideas. Clark and MacCreaigh's *Library Services to the Incarcerated* offers a wealth of advice and know-how on prison libraries, as do Rubin and Suvak's and Vogel's practical guides, although these do not offer a lot of specific advice for juvenile detention libraries.

This book tries to portray what it means to be a librarian for troubled kids who are locked up, some of them for most of their adolescent years, a situation that is often difficult to comprehend, let alone consider objectively. In terms of the pressing need of this population for better access to books and reading, this book is also an exposition of the social justice dimension of the work these librarians do, not only quietly and without fanfare but also, more often, in spite of formidable barriers. I hope this book inspires you to get out and look around your community for those who need better access to books and reading. We know our social services agencies struggle to meet the needs of their constituents; librarians can and should contribute their help. I hope you will be inspired and energized to take on some of this work.

NOTE

1. As of this writing, the author is in the process of conducting the first comprehensive national survey of library services to juveniles in detention, supported by an American Library Association Diversity Research Grant.

Acknowledgments

I can't imagine working with a group of more motivated, caring, and simply great people who agreed to be interviewed for this project. They gave generously of their time and shared their thoughts, sent me all sorts of documentation and links, and even invited me to visit. I am so fortunate to have had the chance to talk with you about what you do, and I thank you all:

Blair Austin (Colorado Youthful Offender System, Pueblo Complex), Rachel Bernstein (San Francisco Public Library at Juvenile Justice Center), Amy Cheney (Write to Read, Juvenile Justice Center, Alameda County Library), Jessica Fenster-Sparber (Passages Academy), Margo Fesperman (Mecklenberg County Sheriff's Office), Deidra Herring (Ohio State University Libraries), Lisa Hussey (Simmons College, Graduate School of Library and Information Science), Dale Jenne (Log Cabin Ranch School, San Francisco Public Library), Melissa Jensen (Platte Valley Youth Services Center Library), Patrick Jones (Hennepin County Library), Anja Kennedy (Passages Academy—Summit), Lindsay Klick (UCLA Nidorf Project), Jennifer Lawson (San Diego County Library), Maria Lowe (Gregory Heights Library, Multnomah County Library), Ya-Ling Lu (Rutgers University, Department of Library and Information Science), Erica MacCreaigh (Colorado State Library), Kathy McLellan (Johnson County Library), Susan Minobe (UCLA Graduate School of Education and Information Studies), Bill Mongelli (San Jose State University, School of Library and Information Science), Jill Morrison (King County Library System), Kevin Murray (Beaumont Juvenile Correctional Center), Kate Pickett (Johnson County Library), Roberta Reasoner (Juvenile Services Education Program, Maryland State Department of Education), and Chuck Steinbower (Scioto Juvenile Correctional Facility).

I have a theory about what happens when you are interviewed about your work (or anything you care about). I think that these kinds of interviews, if you are the interviewee, make you stop and think in a different way about your job and the implications of what you do every day. Where you want your programs to go, what improvements need to be made, and how to go about making those happen. In the very challenging environment of juvenile corrections, I think it's safe to say there will always be room for improvements. So much more needs to be done to nurture the literacy and development of the youth you work with. I really hope that through contributing to this project, you have been able to develop some new ideas and perhaps even have had an "aha" moment or two that will help your services along.

Introduction

WHY THIS BOOK

This book reports on a research project on library services to juveniles in detention. On any given day, close to 92,000 teens, preteens, and young adults are currently detained in this country, most of them from disadvantaged and minority groups, and many having experienced poverty, violence, and neglect (Sickmund, Sladky, and Kang 2008). Library service to these at-risk young people is vital, and yet they are one of our least-served populations. Although exact numbers are difficult to come by, evidence suggests that many residential facilities housing young people do not provide adequate access to library services, books, or programs that would educate and foster positive change for these young people. Librarians and others who serve in these environments confront daily impediments in providing even the most basic services to a population with complex and urgent needs while coping with the many troubling paradoxes of serving within the juvenile justice system.

Providing access to books and reading for detained youth is perhaps one of the last true frontiers in library service. While prison libraries have been around for some time (in this country, they first appeared roughly 200 years ago), libraries for incarcerated juveniles have not. The practice of detaining children for wrongdoing or protection is not new either, but education for these youth was mandated in this country only in the mid-1970s (Dohrn 2002; Rosenheim et al. 2002). While the American Library Association (ALA) has pledged to support library services to youth in detention, these facilities are not required to provide access to reading materials for their residents, nor are libraries required by the standards for correctional education for juveniles (Correctional Education Association 2004). Library service to juveniles in detention is still in its infancy.

The purpose of the study was to discover and document certain basic information about library services to detained youth, specifically to answer questions such as "How much access do youth in detention have to books and reading?" "What kinds of reading guidance, programming, and literacy assistance do youth need, and how much do they receive?" "What are the benefits of reading for this particular group?" And "How can services be improved?"

A preliminary exploration in the literature and interviews with librarians uncovered numerous problems that need attention. These issues reach beyond basic concerns such as the sheer lack of library collections and services in many institutions, insufficient resources, lack of trained staff, and inadequate facility space. Even where library services do exist, adequate access to books and programming is often thwarted by institutional characteristics peculiar to the detention environment. Youth can be restricted from visiting their libraries or denied access to reading materials in their cells depending on security conditions. Popular reading materials can be censored inordinately despite the existence of agreed-upon collection policies. Access to computers can be restricted or denied based on local administrative policies. Volunteers bringing in books and programs can be denied entry depending on security conditions. And, on a higher level, facility rules and policies can change frequently and without notice.

Evidence in the study suggests that the nature of communication, cooperation, and collaboration among librarians, corrections administrators, and staff is central to how well these problems are addressed or if they are addressed at all. Libraries within adult correctional facilities have always had areas of conflict with parent correctional institutions, and the same is true in juvenile detention institutions. Libraries provide access to information, education, and recreational reading for detained youth, while security concerns often must limit that access in various ways. Librarian cooperation with corrections personnel, particularly in terms of adhering to security rules, has long been recognized as essential in meeting library objectives. However, there is much more to library services in the juvenile justice environment.

WHAT'S IN THE BOOK

I discovered early on in this project that not only was very little known about libraries in detention, but also even less seemed to be known (in the library world, at least) about juvenile detention institutions themselves, about how youth get there, or about the special problems and needs of these young people. To that end, Chapter 1 describes briefly the history of juvenile justice and youth detention in the United States, and explains how some of the early juvenile detention schools and libraries got started. Chapter 2 sketches out the basic steps in the juvenile justice process and introduces some of the vocabulary used in the juvenile system. Different types of juvenile facilities in current use are also described.

Chapter 3 introduces the youth themselves: first, who are they and why are they there? Demographic and statistical information illustrates some of the broad characteristics of juveniles in detention, including age, race and ethnicity, and custody rates by state. Mental health, substance abuse, and other special behavioral and cognitive issues associated with many juveniles in detention are covered. The chapter closes with a discussion on how these characteristics help us understand the special information needs of this group.

Chapter 4 explores some of the many facets of information services offered to youth in detention. It focuses on the unique attributes of reader's advisory, information literacy instruction, and library programming in the detention environment.

Libraries and services are not necessarily provided the same way from facility to facility, however, so Chapter 5 continues with descriptions of the most common service models, including the school library media center and the public library branch models, services to living unit collections, and outreach services. Other administrative information such as the role of support personnel from state libraries, the use of service agreements, and different collection access and organization models is discussed.

Chapter 6 describes a number of exemplary programs and services in current use. Chapter 7 explores some of the perplexing issues surrounding collection development for juveniles in detention, and provides guidance for surmounting some of the hurdles associated with censorship and access in detention libraries.

Chapter 8 addresses the role of the library in relation to the rest of the detention facility, particularly as it relates to communication and cooperation between the library and the other agencies in the juvenile system that the library has to work with. In Chapter 9, I close with some words on how to advance the purpose and function of libraries in juvenile detention by focusing on the library's potential role in contributing to the balanced and restorative justice goals of child welfare and juvenile justice.

Two appendices contain supplemental material that will be of use to the practitioner. Appendix A provides three model library-facility service agreements from libraries with different service models (public library versus school library, for example). Appendix B contains useful resources, online and otherwise, on advocacy for youth and reading, collection development, juvenile justice, and programming.

NOTES ON THE RESEARCH

This study began as a qualitative exploration to discover the breadth of library services to juveniles in detention in the United States. While there exists a thin but arguably comprehensive body of literature on adult prison libraries, there is very little written specifically about services to detained juveniles. The overall research questions for this exploration centered on several broad areas: services offered; staffing and funding; information-related needs of this user group; major issues and challenges in the current detention environment; and knowledge, skills, and personal characteristics needed for service providers.

My intent in this exploration was to capture an overall picture of the current state of library services rather than to cover each of these topics in detail. A two-phase study design eventually emerged to collect two types of information: 1) descriptive information on library services, and 2) quantitative measures on the extent of those services in facilities nationally via a survey. This report presents information collected in the first phase of the study.

I sought out interviews with librarians and library services providers, public library outreach coordinators, state library institutional consultants, and volunteers involved with bringing reading materials and/or library-related programming into detention facilities. I solicited participants mainly through e-mail invitations sent to two key e-mail lists for this population, YALSA-LOCKDOWN and PRISON-L.[1] I asked the initial respondents to suggest additional people who might want to participate, and I contacted those individuals by e-mail as well. I found a third group of service providers through the literature review and invited them to participate via e-mail.

I talked with a total of 24 participants in telephone interviews lasting about one to two hours each, and these were recorded and transcribed. Several key participants contributed additional time for a series of more in-depth interviews. A few participants invited me to visit, and I was able to visit two detention facilities, one in California and one in Washington State. I used the ATLAS.ti™ qualitative software program to code and analyze transcripts, notes, and memos.

The literature review covered a broad range of issues related to library services in juvenile detention, including:

- the history and current state of library services and programs in juvenile detention facilities;
- aspects of the juvenile justice system, process, and history relevant to libraries;
- standards and guidelines related to juvenile corrections, libraries, and correctional education; and
- reading and literacy issues relating to juveniles in detention and at-risk youth.

A note on terminology: For the sake of brevity, "detention center," "corrections facility," "residential program," and other similar terms are used interchangeably to refer generally to facilities that youth are housed in. In the juvenile justice system, these different types of facilities have different purposes and characteristics (briefly described in Chapter 2), which could have local implications for library services. These specific cases are noted where necessary.

NOTE

1. YALSA-LOCKDOWN is coordinated by the Young Adult Library Services Association (YALSA), a division of the American Library Association (ALA). PRISON-L is coordinated by the Association of Specialized and Cooperative Libraries Association (ASCLA), also an ALA division.

I

"A Perpetual Tug of War": Conflicting Paradigms in Juvenile Detention

> Your prohibition of all books, letters and papers for the use of convicts, save the Bible and temperance almanacs, is absolutely hellish, abominable, damnable. I wish I knew what fiend devised this cruelty.
>
> —William Joseph Snelling, *The Rat-Trap, or, Cogitations of a Convict in the House of Correction* (1837)

Adult prison libraries have existed in this country in some form or another for over 200 years. The same cannot be said for libraries in juvenile detention centers. The truth is that we know very little about the history of libraries for the use of youth in detention, and we know only slightly more about the extent of these library services today.

This exploration therefore begins with what we do know. We have a substantial base of knowledge on how juvenile detention itself evolved, for example, as well as some evidence about the public's historical perception of the role of books, libraries, and education in detention. This chapter presents a brief history of juvenile detention and introduces what is known about the origins of concepts of education and library service for young people who are detained in these facilities.[1]

A BRIEF HISTORY OF JUVENILE DETENTION IN THE UNITED STATES

Today's juvenile detention centers in the United States are products of opposing perspectives on juvenile justice, what has been referred to as a "perpetual tug-of-war" between rehabilitation and punishment (Springer and Roberts 2009). Rehabilitation presumes that the youth is a work in progress, whose development and behavior are influenced by his or her environment, and whose blame is limited due to age and inexperience. The goal of rehabilitation is to help the child learn to live and behave appropriately in the world.

The punitive approach, on the other hand, presumes the child is deficient in some way, and so must be prevented from inflicting harm on society. The dual goals of punishment are to protect society from the offender and to punish the offender for bad behavior (Maloney, Romig, and Armstrong 1988).

In the late 1980s, an alternative philosophy began to emerge to challenge these opposing perspectives. *Balanced and restorative justice* principles focus on the need for holding youths accountable for their actions, to work with the victims and communities to make amends, and to help youths develop skills and competencies to enable them to be better citizens (Singer 2009). Balanced and restorative justice has been offered as an alternative to help address the limitations of juvenile justice approaches at either end of the rehabilitation-punishment spectrum. Punishment alone fails because the offender has no opportunity to develop empathy or self-control. Rehabilitation alone fails to hold the offender accountable for his or her actions, and excuses bad behavior rather than addressing root causes. Balanced and restorative justice seeks an equal emphasis across these approaches.

While the U.S. Department of Justice Office of Juvenile Justice Delinquency Prevention (OJJDP) has embraced restorative justice principles, and a majority of institutions currently include them in their mission statements, it is difficult to assess to what extent this relatively new framework has influenced either the conditions of juvenile detention or its outcomes. It is important to recognize that all approaches to juvenile justice, whether punitive, rehabilitative, or restorative, have particular salience for library services to incarcerated youth.

These underlying philosophies are introduced here at the beginning to shed some light on the fundamental and historical tensions underlying the basic rationale of detaining youth, because these tensions exist today and they affect library services on many levels. It is important to understand how these conflicting paradigms have developed, and how they have influenced library operations within detention facilities.

Children wind up in detention today for a range of reasons. Youth might be arrested for committing serious crimes such as robbery or assault, or for less serious "status" offenses such as truancy, violating curfew, or running away. Some abused or neglected children end up in the system because they cannot be placed elsewhere; perhaps they have run away from a foster home or have been removed from a placement because of behavior issues. This is how it stands today, and the historical evolution of facilities to house neglected or offending children reflects the multiple natures and causes of these circumstances. The history of child welfare and institutional treatment of children is beyond the scope of this book, but it is important to note that child welfare and juvenile justice policies have shifted substantially and regularly over time, along with public sentiment toward juvenile crime, and continue to do so. A general understanding of these conditions provides context for understanding how libraries developed within these systems, and how they have come to be what they are today.

THE HOUSES OF REFUGE

The first institutions created specifically to house delinquent or neglected juveniles in the United States opened in the early decades of the nineteenth century as alternatives to the adult jails, prisons, almshouses, and workhouses that housed all persons guilty of many offenses. Research by the Society for the Prevention of Pauperism in New York into the deplorable state of the city's penitentiaries, which at the time housed both adult and juvenile prisoners, was instrumental in establishing a separate facility for juveniles, the New York House of Refuge, in 1825 (New York State Archives). An 1822 report outlined the rehabilitative philosophy for the House of Refuge:

These prisons should be schools of instruction rather than places of punishment like our state prisons. The youth confined there should be placed under a course of discipline.... The end should be his reformation and future usefulness. (Snedden 1907)

The Society's mission was reinforced by their adoption of a new name in 1824, the Society for the Reformation of Juvenile Delinquents. It is important to note that both criminal (i.e., delinquent) youth as well as youths who were simply homeless, vagrant, and/or destitute were detained here. From its earliest times, detention served this dual purpose: as punishment for a range of bad behaviors as well as refuge for neglected youth with nowhere else to go. In addition to referral from law enforcement, youths could be committed by their parents, by city aldermen under the doctrine of *parens patriae*, or by the authority of the state to assume wardship of a child if the parents were deemed unfit. Youth were committed to the House of Refuge until age 21, regardless of the nature of the offense or situation.

Six boys and three girls were the first detainees in the New York House of Refuge, and by the end of 1825, 73 children had been received, most of whom were poor or dependent rather than criminal or delinquent. Within a decade, 1,678 inmates were admitted, and by 1855 two new facilities were built. Other houses of refuge soon opened in Boston, Baltimore, Philadelphia, Chicago, St. Louis, and New Orleans. Separate facilities were eventually established for girls and some for children of color, although several facilities remained integrated, notably in New York, Boston, and California. Funding for these refuges came from both public and private monies; administration was most often left in the hands of private philanthropic organizations.

As construction and operation of these houses of refuge spread across the country, the growing need for more space, staff, and services made continuing private oversight untenable. Eventually, some state and local governments took over administration and funding for some schools, while others remained private.

INDUSTRIAL SCHOOLS, TRAINING SCHOOLS, AND REFORMATORIES

Other detention facilities in the mid-nineteenth century were designed as "industrial schools," training schools, or reformatories, with the goal of providing smaller cottage-like environments for 25 to 30 youths each, with vocational training, academic schooling, and a "disciplined environment." In reality, the schooling provided was barely minimal, vocational training amounted to facility maintenance work, and discipline was often harsh and punitive.

Although the point was to save children from the horrid conditions in the adult jails and workhouses, conditions in most of the reform schools and refuges were as deplorable as or worse than those of the adult facilities. Overcrowding and illness were endemic. Despite the conditions, however, the notion had been established by the mid- to late nineteenth century that juveniles should be treated differently than adults in terms of their delinquency and welfare. Juveniles could now be physically separated from adults within a correctional facility or held in a facility specifically for juveniles, be removed from their families and detained, or be assessed via a separate legal system (the soon-to-be juvenile court), which determined not only guilt or innocence but also custody, disposition, and treatment intended in "the best interest of the child."

TWENTIETH-CENTURY JUVENILE DETENTION

The first juvenile court in this country came into being in Cook County, Illinois, in 1899, at the end of a turbulent decade of debate over the role of public intervention in the lives of juveniles (Tanenhaus 2002). By that time, there were essentially three types of institutions for coping with troubled youth: adult jails and prisons, training schools and reformatories, and private houses of refuge and similar facilities. Although jails, prisons, and training schools and reformatories were intended to serve a corrections function, and houses of refuge to help poverty-stricken children, families, and unwed mothers, in reality all three institutions often housed delinquent as well as dependent children.

In response to continued pressure from social reformers, by 1923 there were significantly fewer juveniles being admitted to adult institutions. Census data indicate that for the year 1923 (the first year for which data on these facilities are available), over 33,000 juveniles were admitted to juvenile facilities, with a "census day" count of 1,489 (Lerman 2002). These facilities were modeled on jails, with barred windows and locked doors, and were commonly staffed by political appointees with no particular training in corrections or child development. As in the reform schools and refuges, juveniles were housed in these facilities for a number of reasons in addition to criminal behavior, including truancy, incorrigibility, and neglect.

The Social Security Act of 1935 authorized federal expenditures for the Aid to Dependent Children program (later known as Aid to Families with Dependent Children, or AFDC), offering aid for the care of neglected children in their own homes or in foster care. This legislation served to shift a substantial amount of funds away from institutions and essentially eliminated the need for the remaining houses of refuge, orphanages, almshouses, and workhouses (Lerman 2002).

Not surprisingly, the incarceration of children increased during the Great Depression of the 1930s. By the 1940s, although brutal conditions in juvenile detention facilities were commonly reported, a lack of staffing and resources due to the war hampered reform. After World War II, public sentiment began to display a preference for housing and treating youth with more serious behavioral problems, now called "emotionally disturbed," in private residential facilities, many using the same orphanage buildings formerly used for dependent or neglected youth in the prior century. Similar conditions persisted through the 1950s and 1960s.

CAMPS, RANCHES, AND COMMUNITY-BASED CORRECTIONS

Beginning in the 1950s, state and local probation authorities began looking for alternatives to these juvenile detention institutions. Forestry camps and ranches sprang up, particularly in California in the 1950s and 1960s (Lerman 2002). The 1960s and 1970s saw a movement in the juvenile justice system toward "community-based corrections," in which minor offenders such as status and other nondelinquent offenders were housed separately from more serious criminal delinquents. In practice, this amounted to segregating serious offenders in public state corrections facilities, while status offenders and neglected youth were directed to smaller, often private halfway houses, group homes, and similar facilities within local communities. These community-based residential facilities were (and continue to be) characterized by a rehabilitative approach to juvenile treatment, including strict supervision and close monitoring, as well as providing life skills counseling, job placement services, and drug or substance abuse treatment.

1970s AND 1980s: FROM REFORMATION TO PUNISHMENT

In re Gault (1967) was a landmark U.S. Supreme Court decision that established a juvenile's right to due process, including the right to counsel, the right to be informed of charges, and the right to confront witnesses (Shepherd 2003). While helping to protect accused juveniles from biased and unfair judgments, the *Gault* decision was one of a series of judicial decisions that ultimately served to shift the focus of juvenile detention away from rehabilitation and back to punishment. Through the 1980s and 1990s, a rise in juvenile arrest rates for violent crime corresponded with a shift in public opinion about the increasingly dangerous nature of juvenile crime and fostered a correspondingly punitive response (Zimring 2002). Hundreds of new juvenile halls were opened in this period (Figure 1.1).

This shift in public opinion was felt in three areas. First, juvenile delinquents were increasingly viewed as incorrigible, or incapable of reform, resulting in a deemphasis on rehabilitation as a treatment mode. Second, the juvenile justice system was itself deemed increasingly inadequate to cope with the violent nature of juvenile crime, and thus transfer of juveniles to the adult criminal court was viewed as not only acceptable but also necessary. Finally, juvenile delinquency was felt to be a choice of free will, and not a result of neglect, poverty, lack of education, or other socioeconomic or environmental forces. These shifts in assumptions about juvenile delinquency resulted in longer

Figure 1.1

Number of juvenile halls by date of opening

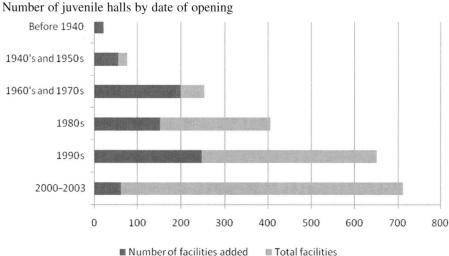

■ Number of facilities added   ■ Total facilities

Source: American Correctional Association. 2003. *National juvenile detention directory.* Lanham, MD: American Correctional Association.

Figure 1.2
Balanced and restorative justice model

Source: Singer, Jonathan B. 2009. From Augustus to BARJ: The evolving role of social work in juvenile justice. In *Handbook of forensic mental health with victims and offenders: Assessment, treatment, and research*, edited by D. W. Springer and A. D. Roberts. New York: Springer.

terms of probation, longer detention, and more transfers to adult criminal corrections as the courts began placing more emphasis on protecting society rather than "acting in the best interest of the child."

Juvenile crime rates began to decline in the mid-1990s, and they continue to do so, albeit gradually. There have been indications of a shift to a new paradigm, *balanced and restorative justice*, a significant alternative to the rehabilitation–punishment dichotomy. Restorative justice principles focus on offender accountability, community involvement, and successful reentry into society.

Balanced and restorative justice concepts began emerging in the 1970s and 1980s based on research indicating that victim restitution and community engagement with youth helped lower recidivism (Maloney, Romig, and Armstrong 1988). In essence, the restorative justice model moves away from punishment versus treatment of problematic behaviors (which often conflict with each other in practice) by engaging the offender in positive, constructive behaviors such as paying restitution to the victim and performing community service, and also provides learning experiences to help offenders gain skills and competencies to enable them to succeed when they reenter society. Restorative justice programs also steer away juvenile justice staff from office-based casework and involve them more in direct engagement with youth and the community.

The restorative justice model relies on three elements—community safety, account-ability, and competency development—all of which must be addressed together (Figure 1.2). These elements are achieved through the following types of mechanisms (Clark County (WA) Juvenile Court 2008; Singer 2009):

- Victims are acknowledged and receive meaningful assistance.
- Victims have the opportunity to participate in the resolution of the crime.
- The community is actively engaged in holding offenders accountable.
- Offenders are held accountable in ways that provide them with opportunity to change and develop into healthy, positive members of the community.
- The community is engaged with supporting the development of offenders' competency to reenter society as a productive citizen.

At this point in time, restorative justice has been promoted by the OJJDP as a national, system-wide improvement, spurred by intensive federally funded training and technical assistance programs. Adapting juvenile codes and administrative procedures to include balanced and restorative concepts has been a complex task, yet interest in restorative justice continues to grow. Most states have incorporated restorative justice principles into their juvenile justice codes (Griffin and Torbet 2002: 12)

Recent court rulings indicate a change in perceptions of punishment as well. In 2005, the U.S. Supreme Court determined that capital punishment was unconstitutional for youth under the age of 18 (Liptak 2009); in 2010, the Supreme Court determined that life imprisonment for nonviolent crimes by youth under age 18 was cruel and unusual punishment and therefore unconstitutional (Liptak 2010). Recognizing that many young delinquent offenders have been "mishandled" by the adult court systems, many state courts are raising the age of adulthood in order to prosecute fewer teenagers as adults (Secret 2011). Many of these changes have been supported by studies concluding that typical older adolescents do not have the same capacity as adults for decision making, and would therefore benefit more from treatment rather than incarceration.

Despite these recent indications of changes in juvenile justice perspectives, conditions in most detention and treatment facilities remain deficient at best. A 1998 report from the OJJDP reiterated its view that youth are subjected to "increasingly overcrowded and significantly deficient facilities . . . [with] abusive and unlawful conditions of confinement [including] deficiencies in living space, security, control of suicidal behavior, health care, education and treatment services," and that these conditions serve only to increase recidivism and violence (Puritz and Scale 1998). A 2009 report from a task force in New York State found that young people battling mental illness or addiction were routinely held alongside criminal offenders in youth prisons where they were physically abused and rarely received counseling, education, or treatment (Confessore 2009). Despite the promising steps forward in implementing competency building through restorative justice programs, the overall state of the current juvenile detention environment remains dire.

A BRIEF HISTORY OF EDUCATION IN DETENTION

Work and education were generally viewed as the primary forces for reforming youth, and so vocational as well as academic and religious education were core components in the houses of refuge and the early training schools and reformatories established in Chicago, New York, Boston, and Philadelphia in the mid-1800s. The first superintendents of these schools were in fact progressive educators, and they eschewed the bars and locks of detention facilities:

[B]oys under a certain age, who become subject to the notice of our police . . . may be received [and] put to work at such employments as will tend to encourage industry and ingenuity, taught reading, writing, and arithmetic, and most carefully instructed in the nature of their moral and religious obligations. . . . [We] hold out every possible inducement to reformation and good conduct. (*Christian Register*, October 1, 1825)

The definition of "education" varied, however, from strictly religious and moral education, to vocational training, to basic instruction in letters and numbers, and to broader course instruction in English, math, music, and geography (which were more or less equivalent to public school offerings).

Given that most of these institutions, both adult and juvenile, were only partially funded by public and private funds, the balance of funds needed was often raised by the sale of products produced by inmate labor. Thus, the ratio of work to education varied as well, with most facilities likely dedicating more hours to work than to vocational training or academic education.

Certainly a high percentage of incarcerated youths and adults in the eighteenth and nineteenth centuries could not read. Literacy at this time could simply mean the ability to write one's name, or read basic messages or passages from the Bible (Ciment 2006). Evidence shows low or absent literacy in the houses of refuge: "On conversing with upwards of twenty boys . . . I found that seventeen of these youthful delinquents were unable to read" (*Christian Herald*, May 31, 1817).

Curious evidence of early reading interventions in adult detention is available, although it is impossible to know how widespread these practices were. The *Christian Herald and Seaman's Magazine* of November 3, 1821, reported on some efforts to teach reading to prisoners:

[T]wenty-two sent in their names as desirous to receive instruction, and one volunteered his services to teach. . . . [A]ll the prisoners . . . were examined . . . and it appeared there were but ten wholly unable to read. . . . Of the ten scholars who could not read in January . . . learned in a few weeks to read in the Testament and Prayer-book, with considerable facility.

Similar progress in teaching reading to younger detainees was reported in the *American Sunday School Magazine* in January 1827:

[M]easures were taken to ascertain the number of convicts who were unable to read. . . . Fifty . . . whose ages did not exceed 25 years . . . were selected and placed in the [Sunday] school. Some could read indifferently well, while others were even ignorant of the alphabet. . . . [I]t is very gratifying to be able to state, that their progress has exceeded the most sanguine expectations.

It was apparent that peer tutoring in one location also enabled prisoners to learn to read:

He was reading a work which had a peculiar interest for him, as it was written in prison, and seemed particularly suited to his wants. . . . [W]e recollected that he could not read when he was on trial and we felt anxious to know how he had accomplished the task of learning to read. . . . [A]nother prisoner . . . was confined in an adjoining cell. He could read, and the clergyman who attended on him left with him a bible. . . . [I]t was determined that the unlettered man should, if possible, have the benefit of reading. He was supplied with a bible. . . . The one who could read, opened his bible to the same place, and read the verse slowly; he then read the first two words, and his pupil in the next cell repeated the same frequently and afterwards found the same words in other verses. (*Hazard's Register of Pennsylvania*, October 10, 1835)

So although it was clear that the reformers at the turn of the twentieth century believed that youth in detention should be afforded education and reading materials, educational offerings and resources such as libraries did not appear to be widely available. Conditions in these schools as of the 1930s were as dismal and repressive as ever, overcrowded, and with untrained and overworked staff (Dohrn 2002). Schooling, where provided, was still only offered for half-days or less. Rare exceptions such as the Cook County Juvenile Temporary Detention Center provided a full-time school run by a board of education. In most facilities, reading materials, if available at all, were often limited to discarded magazines and newspapers.

Schooling in detention facilities was not legally mandated until the mid-1970s. By that time, the Juvenile Justice and Delinquency Prevention Act (JJDPA) effected the first of what many hoped were needed changes, finally acknowledging the need to remove status offenders from correctional facilities and delinquent children from adult jails (Dohrn 2002). During the Reagan presidency, however, the focus of the OJJDP was directed away from prevention and rehabilitation and toward incarceration and punishment of juvenile criminals. In that environment of "getting tough" with youth, the social needs of confined delinquents, including education, had taken a backseat.

THE JUVENILE JUSTICE AND DELINQUENCY PREVENTION ACT

The Juvenile Justice and Delinquency Prevention Act of 1974 (JJDPA) is a federal law providing funds to states that follow a series of federal protections, known as the "core protections," on the care and treatment of youth in the justice system. The four core protections of the act are:

- Deinstitutionalization of status offenders (DSO) requires that youth who are runaways, truants, or curfew violators cannot be detained in juvenile detention facilities or adult jails.
- Jail removal does not permit the placement of youth in adult jails and lockups except under very limited circumstances.
- Sight and sound separation protection does not permit contact between juvenile and adult offenders. If juveniles are put in an adult jail or lockup under the limited circumstances the law allows for, they must be separated from adult inmates.
- The disproportionate minority confinement (DMC) provision requires states to address the issue of overrepresentation of youth of color in the justice system.

The DSO and sight and sound protections were part of the original law in 1974. The jail removal provision was added in 1980 in response to findings that youth incarcerated in adult facilities suffered from "a high suicide rate, physical, mental, and sexual assault, inadequate care and programming, negative labeling, and exposure to serious offenders and mental patients." The DMC requirement was added to the JJDPA in 1992.

The compliance of states toward the requirements of the JJDPA is monitored by the OJJDP. As of November 2008, a vast majority of states and territories comply with JJDPA requirements (OJJDP 2008).

Adapted from: Citizens for Juvenile Justice (CfJJ): http://www.cfjj.org/jjdpa.html

---

In 2005, the Standards Commission of the Correctional Education Association (CEA) approved a separate set of standards for accrediting correctional educational programs in juvenile facilities. These standards focus on making sure students in detention are provided the same level of educational programming as students outside. The amount of time spent in the classroom must meet at least the minimum required by state regulations, and special education needs must be identified and provided for. Education records must be provided to the facility as soon as possible to help assess student placement.

The main goal of juvenile correctional education is for students to earn a high school diploma or general equivalency diploma (GED); most programs strive to grant credits that are acceptable to students' high schools outside. Teachers must be certified in the subjects they teach. However, while the fact that these standards exist is a positive development for meeting youths' educational needs, evidence in this study suggests that actual programs in detention are very different from high schools outside. Many factors challenge educational delivery in detention, particularly the high proportion of students with mental health and behavioral disorders and the very low literacy rates. Security concerns often prevent students from having access to pens or pencils outside the classroom, so "doing homework" outside of class time is not possible, further minimizing the amount of time students have available to engage in learning activities.

Today, although every state requires education for incarcerated children, schooling in most juvenile detention facilities continues to fail on many levels, according to the OJJDP (Puritz and Scale 1998). Resources are lacking and qualified teachers are scarce. It is difficult enough for students to come into a classroom in the middle of the curriculum; these difficulties are compounded with dozens of students at different levels of learning, many with mental health and behavioral problems, and many with special education needs. Many residents were not attending school regularly before their incarceration; most read well below grade level at the time they are detained. The regular activities of the facility (lockdowns, punishment, transfers, and court hearings) disrupt class time. Correctional staff and administrators often have priorities that are different from those of educators.

LIBRARIES IN JUVENILE DETENTION

Coyle's history of prison libraries offers an excellent analysis of the social conditions that shaped adult prison libraries for the first two centuries of U.S. history (Coyle 1987). In contrast, very little is known about libraries in the early houses of refuge during the nineteenth century. Popular periodicals of the day provide only a glimpse of the libraries in one reformatory school and two adult prisons, highlighting the usefulness of libraries for education as well as behavior management, and the use of private donations for funding.

In the New York House of Refuge:

Four hours of each day are spent in their schools where they are instructed in all the elementary branches of practical education—and a library, with globes and maps, has recently been purchased. The children, in general, pursue their studies with zeal, and the volumes of the library are read with avidity. (*Christian Advocate*, March 3, 1827)

In the Ohio Penitentiary in Columbus:

This library, containing about 7000 volumes, has been mainly procured . . . [by] soliciting books and funds from the citizens of the State. [A] gasometer has been constructed . . . so that every prisoner can spend his evenings in reading rather than in profitless gloom and solitude. The result has proved most satisfactory. (*The Independent*, April 19, 1849)

In the Elmira (New York) Reformatory:

One of the best features in this reformatory is compulsory education, and the attendant marks, which affect the terms of imprisonment.... They have a circulating library ... and one reads with interest and curiosity the list of authors most read: Charles Dickens, Alex. Dumas, Rider Haggard, Edna Lyall, Bulwer Lytton.... [I]t seems to me a fair showing of good taste in novel reading, though probably if the most sensational order were furnished they would be in demand. (Chapman 1894)

By the turn of the twentieth century, professional library literature began to address the role of books, reading, and libraries specifically for detained youth in more detail. Juvenile reform school libraries were often discussed together with other institutional libraries serving the range of state institutions caring for the "insane, the defective, the criminal, and the unfortunate" (Carey 1907b). The chief goal of the reform school library was the "fostering and creation of the reading habit" by means of children's books and "easy books" using simple language, large clear type, and plenty of pictures. Collections were to be "miscellaneous in character but have reference to the special requirements of [their] own readers." Librarians also felt that girls and boys had differ-ent reading needs:

The library of an orphan's home should consist of children's books, for a girls' reformatory school, books of out-door life and adventure should predominate, with as little as possible of the emotional. The boys' reformatory needs, in addition to a good all-around collection, works on the useful arts. (Carey 1907b)

It is important to note that even at this early stage, attention was being paid to the needs and interests of the individual, as well as to the role of the librarian and teacher in encouraging reading by being "that vital link between the book and the reader." These are key characteristics of juvenile detention libraries that have influenced library services and that persist to this day.

Personal attention may not have meant "in person" attention, however. A superinten-dent of schools in Indiana described a library that "must serve a patronage that can not [sic] come in person to the library and make a personal choice ... the librarian can not come into personal contact with the reader" (Asbury 1907). To address this limitation, the Indiana Reformatory Library devised a process for classifying every individual by reading level, in order to help the librarian select appropriate material when the prisoner did not choose appropriate reading material for himself.

In 1905, Iowa was the first state to create a position for a "supervising librarian" to periodically visit institutional libraries, establish records, introduce classification sys-tems, and train assistants. Other states followed suit in subsequent years. (Today, many states employ state library institutional consultants who serve similar functions.)

By 1935, *Library Journal* was publishing infrequent but regular accounts of libraries in orphanages and reform schools. Branch pointed out around this time that one of the most demanding characteristics of the orphanage library was its need to function both as a school library during classroom hours and as a public library in the evenings and on weekends—a practice and a challenge that continue today in many facilities (Branch 1935).

Library work was occasionally offered to older children as part of the manual work required of children to help "compensate for [their] maintenance by the state." Library collections by this time had grown beyond school textbooks and recreational reading to include materials on the breadth of work activities, including farming, dairying, carpentry, and mechanical and technical arts, and, for the girls, books on cooking, sewing, laundry, and housework. At the Dr. John de la Howe Industrial School in 1935, the library had room for 30 children and adequate shelves for 2,000 volumes, although there was no card catalog:

The teacher librarian must be very familiar with the titles of all the books and with their subject groupings on the shelves. Registration and book cards have not been found necessary, the ledger system of charging books is used, and the children are easily found and informed that their book has been kept overdue. (Branch 1935)

By 1945, the library program at the National Training School for Boys in Washington, DC, included a library orientation session that covered the library's contents and physical arrangement, and the residents' privileges and responsibilities, stressing its similarity to school and public libraries everywhere. Boys filled out a card with their name, age, and date of arrival, upon which was recorded every book they check out, "for a complete and continuous record of every book he has read during his stay" (Appel 1945). The librarian would read a folk tale or other story at the orientation.

Boys with permits from their teachers visited the library "constantly" to do research for classroom projects; teachers also brought in their classes weekly to check out books for recreational reading. Library "lessons" on the use of the encyclopedia, almanac, and *Readers' Guide* were coordinated with English and social studies classroom activities.

The collections for the boys were specifically developed to meet the "interests of the boys, as determined by their teachers . . . the basic philosophy is a collection that will meet the need and interest of any boy." Published lists were also used to fill out the collection such as *A Basic Book Collection for High Schools* and *Character Formation through Books*. The media collection included sound recordings, films, and filmstrips, and the library regularly rented educational films to accompany the school curriculum. This library also included a professional development collection for the staff, with works on education, sociology, and delinquency. Interlibrary loan was used for obtaining specialized materials "from the varied facilities available in Washington, DC, ie, the Library of Congress."

Boys could earn certificates for reading and reporting on 20 or more books. Older boys could work in the library if they were at least 17 years old and could type and alphabetize.

During the 1940s, the objectives of the reformatory library were also becoming better defined. Institutionalized children as well as adults needed books to help them relax, draw attention away from themselves, and substitute "healthy interests for malformed ones" (Methven 1943). Manuals for library practices were beginning to be compiled in a few locations, and professionals were noting the need for more trained librarians and for closer attention to be paid to each child's individual reading interests. Interest was growing in developing some record of each individual's reading accomplishments, as well as some "carry-over procedure to post-institutional reading activity."

The promise of all this optimism for the future in the 1930s and 1940s did not come to fruition in the following decades, however. A lack of funding and low salaries kept trained librarians away from corrections work in general, and this neglect was magnified in the hundreds of juvenile halls that opened from the 1950s through the 1990s (see Figure 1.1), many of which lacked adequate libraries and educational facilities.

Along with the view during the 1950s that delinquent children were somehow "emotionally disturbed," therapeutic models of treatment for delinquent children were also on the rise beginning in the 1950s. Librarians, teachers, and psychologists were exploring applications of bibliotherapy in juvenile correctional institutions, particularly combining group reading with psychotherapy.

Research on the impact of various types of reading on troubled children and teens expanded librarians' understanding of how books might be used to "change attitudes" (Brown 1975). The emphasis remained on works that were "reasonably well written and had believable characters and situations with which the boys and girls could identify." Lists of books were compiled according to the properties of various types of literature and how they might help (or hinder); books were also classified by the type of problem addressed (such as physical handicaps, drug addiction, and emotional disturbances). Although there was a definite surge in interest in using books to help "straighten out the thinking of a student whose mind has become badly warped," Brown admits that there were not enough librarians, teachers, or psychotherapists to develop adequate individualized bibliotherapy programs in institutional settings.[2]

However, the 1950s saw an emerging understanding of the psychological impacts of detention and its effects on the information needs of children, and this began to sharpen the way librarians viewed reading in this context. Children needed to be able to read to escape, to feel secure, and to learn that their emotional experiences were shared by others:

All children are disturbed by the experience of being locked up whether it is the first time or the twentieth. Whether the child is here because a mother is too ill to care for him temporarily, because he became lost, or because he robbed a home with a gun in his hands, he is beset by fears of what the grownups are going to do to him. He is ridden with anxiety for his immediate future . . . anxiety and uncertainty are never far from the surface and this makes his behavior unpredictable and occasionally explosive. (May 1953)

Interpersonal characteristics of the librarian in juvenile corrections were also becoming better understood. Librarians needed to gain the confidence and trust of the youth, be sensitive to feelings, and be accepting of the individual as a person. In order to be able to suggest appropriate books, the librarian should know the student well, know the material thoroughly, and take time to discuss books with students in a "friendly and informal manner." It was thought that bibliotherapy would be most effective with individuals of average or above-average reading ability.

During the 1940s and 1950s, state library institutional consultants tried to fill the massive gaps in service and to bring some kind of order to neglected collections that mostly comprised donations from charity and religious groups, and establish constructive library programs (Cook 1953). It was an uphill battle. Libraries in the burgeoning juvenile corrections industry were not a priority, even when educators seemed to be willing to support them. The American Correctional Association (ACA) and the Correctional Education Association vocalized the need for librarians, for organized and focused library programs, for appropriate collections rather than miscellaneous donations, and for suitable space and budgets as early as 1963 (Moore and Moore 1963).

Toward the end of the 1970s, librarians became increasingly aware of other characteristics of juveniles in detention: a lack of motivation in school, an increased rate of learning disabilities and behavior problems, and little knowledge of libraries. In addressing these issues, librarians were urged to work with the social workers, teachers, counselors, health professionals, and psychologists to know the students' special "problems and restrictions" and pay personal attention to each youth (Knepel and Knepel 1979). Librarians were also trying harder to make the library more enjoyable with more popular and recreational materials, games, and media.

A survey of correctional libraries published in 1974 by the Institute of Library Research at the University of California, Berkeley documented the severe lack of access to materials and services across the vast majority of adult and juvenile institutions (LeDonne, Christiano, and Scantlebury 1974). The study concluded that the critical factors in need of change were recognition of inmates' right to read, stable funding, and better communication and cooperation between institutions and outside librarians:

Institutional libraries have not kept pace with libraries outside; generally, the concept of library service prevalent among institutional administrators, educators, and librarians is limited, stereotyped, and out of date; and stated library objectives were inconsistent with the stated objectives of the institution. (LeDonne, Christiano, and Scantlebury 1974)

In 1975 the American Correctional Association, in partnership with the Health and Rehabilitative Library Services Division (formerly the Association of Hospital and Institution Libraries) of the American Library Association, produced *Library Standards for Juvenile Correctional Institutions*. Prior to this time, there were no standards or guidelines for library services to juveniles in detention, save for a brief section on "Library Services" in *Institutions Serving Delinquent Children: Guides and Goals*, published by the Children's Bureau of the U.S. Department of Health, Education, and Welfare in 1958, which stated the general purpose and function of the library and encouraged its use:

Library materials should meet informational, inspirational, reference, and recreational needs and provide a positive influence on the formation of personal attitudes and values. It is important that there be a wide variety of materials that do not demand high reading skills. (Children's Bureau 1957)

The basic assumptions for the 1975 standards were that librarians would be directly concerned with the rehabilitation of young offenders, and that library services should recognize the juvenile delinquent's special needs and interests. The guidelines stated that libraries should "support, broaden, and strengthen" the institution's overall mission to rehabilitate young offenders through treatment and education. To that end, librarians were charged to take an "active role" in the overall institutional planning and implementation. The standards provided brief definitions of library terms; the overall mission and scope of library service, including a basic collection policy; the types of services to be offered; and a brief description of personnel qualifications.

The 1975 standards noted new developments in the treatment of delinquent young people, such as increased community involvement with juvenile correction, as well as new developments in library services. The standards stated that services available to communities should be available to juvenile residential facilities, and presumably this would include libraries. However, the standards were intended to be applied only to long-term facilities offering "strong academic-vocational programs," not to short-term detention facilities housing youth for fewer than 60 days.

The Association of Specialized and Cooperative Library Agencies (ASCLA), in cooperation once again with the American Correctional Association, began a revision to the standards in 1987. The impetus for this revision stemmed from several issues. Clearly there was a need to incorporate ongoing developments in library technologies. More importantly, significant changes were occurring in the economic and policy environments in both library services at the federal level as well as juvenile corrections. The passage of the JJDPA in particular served to increase the number of juveniles in the system as well as lengthen their sentences. There was also a growing need to address the impact of increasingly confusing administrative structures in juvenile corrections: responsibility for library services differed from place to place, and could be spread among state and local corrections, public libraries, educational agencies, and state library agencies, resulting in a confusing array of often conflicting policies. Finally, librarians recognized the need to provide services to short-term as well as long-term facilities. The approved revision was published 12 years later in 1999.

Several additional policy documents were appended to the 1999 Standards, including the Library Bill of Rights, Free Access to Libraries for Minors, the Resolution on Prisoner's Right to Read, the Policy on Confidentiality of Library Records, and the Freedom to Read Statement. The Prisoner's Right to Read was updated and reaffirmed in 2010, without any modification to its statement on juveniles in detention.

NOTES

1. Grateful appreciation to Susan Minobe (MLS, UCLA), who contributed substantial research and writing to this chapter.

2. During the 1980s, librarians for the most part seemed to want to disengage from the clinical and psychological aspects of bibliotherapy as a formal practice of recommending books to help people with problems. Librarians were not seen as "qualified" to conduct bibliotherapy as a clinical practice when compared with psychologists and other mental health professionals (Smith 1989). The Bibliotherapy Committee of the American Library Association disbanded early in the 1990s.

2

The Juvenile Justice Process Today

The juvenile justice system today has important differences that set it apart from adult corrections. The first thing to note is that there is no one single juvenile justice system in this country: each state and the District of Columbia has its own rules for dealing with youth who violate the law. To further complicate matters, procedures vary considerably from state to state, and local practices and traditions abound at the community level.

With that in mind, this section summarizes in a general way the process that most youth are likely to experience on their way to being admitted to a detention or placement facility. This process is illustrated in Figure 2.1. The Office of Juvenile Justice and Delinquency Prevention (OJJDP) is a good source for more information on the process across states and localities, as well as federal policies and statistics, with links to state and local information resources and practices (see http://ojjdp.ncjrs.gov/ ojstatbb/ezaucr/). County and municipal Web sites can provide information on locally administered facilities.

Take a Tour of the San Diego County Juvenile Hall on YouTube
http://www.youtube.com/watch?v=f1fVcBfhMCQ&feature=related

FIRST CONTACT: LAW ENFORCEMENT

Most youth come into first contact with the juvenile justice system through law enforcement. Police officers determine whether the youth should be released or detained after talking to the youth, the victim, and the youth's parents, and reviewing prior contacts with the law. About 70 percent of youth who are arrested are referred to juvenile court, and about 30 percent are released.

Figure 2.1
The juvenile justice process

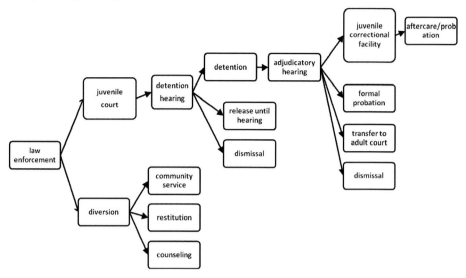

Source: Adapted from Juvenile Justice System Flowchart, Center for Juvenile & Criminal Justice http://www.cjcj.org/juvenile/justice/juvenile/justice/overview and Juvenile Justice in California, 2008, California Department of Justice et al. http://ag.ca.gov/cjsc/pubs.php.

Sometimes juveniles are held in a secure facility for a few hours while parents or guardians are contacted. The Juvenile Justice and Delinquency Prevention Act (JJDPA) discourages law enforcement from detaining youth alongside adults; thus many (but not all) adult jails have holding facilities that separate youth from contact with adults.

JUVENILE COURT INTAKE

If the case is referred to juvenile court, a juvenile probation officer is usually responsible for conducting the court intake procedure. This could include reviewing the facts of the case, and determining whether there is enough evidence to prove the allegation. Some cases are dismissed at this point. Intake determines whether formal intervention is necessary or whether the case could be handled informally. About half of all cases are handled informally and are ultimately dismissed after the youth agrees to certain conditions, such as paying restitution, attending school, observing a curfew, and/or receiving counseling or substance abuse treatment. These conditions are written up in an agreement called a *consent decree*. A probation officer might be responsible for monitoring the youth's compliance for a specified time.

If the youth meets all the requirements of the consent decree, the case is dismissed. If the youth fails to meet the requirements, he or she could be brought back to court to be prosecuted in a formal hearing.

Some youth are held in a secure facility while the case is being processed or while waiting for a hearing, if the court believes it is in the best interest of the community or the youth. These juveniles might be considered a danger to themselves or others, or probation officers determine that they might be likely to not show up at their hearing.

A detention hearing must be held within a specified time period, usually 24 hours, of intake. At the detention hearing, a judge decides whether the juvenile should continue to be detained prior to adjudication (the juvenile justice version of a trial). About 21 percent of juveniles are detained prior to adjudication.

ADJUDICATION

If the case is filed in juvenile court, the prosecutor can file one of two types of petitions: delinquency or waiver. For a delinquency petition, an adjudicatory hearing is scheduled, which is essentially a trial where the facts are presented, witnesses are called, and a judge determines whether the youth is delinquent. In some places, a jury trial can be requested. Youth are *adjudicated* delinquent (guilty) in about two-thirds of all cases that get this far. (Note that the language used in juvenile court filings is different from that used in adult proceedings: juveniles are *adjudicated* and *placed*, while adults are *tried and sentenced*.)

Some juvenile cases are waived and transferred to adult criminal court. This can happen for a number of reasons, such as if the charges are serious enough, or if the juvenile has committed prior serious offenses or repeatedly violated probation. That decision is usually made by the prosecutor and the judge. In some states, the upper age limit for juvenile offenses is as low as 15. In those cases, a waiver petition is filed, in which the juvenile court waives jurisdiction for the case and sends the case to adult criminal court. Some juvenile offenders, at age 15, are tried as adults.

Although the number of states that require certain juveniles to be tried as adults had grown over the years, some states have recently reduced the scope of those laws, transferring fewer juveniles. A recent study indicated that transferring youth to the adult criminal court has not reduced recidivism, and has in fact increased the likelihood of reoffending, particularly for violent crimes (Redding 2010).

DISPOSITION

After adjudication, a disposition hearing is scheduled, in which the probation officer submits a set of recommendations for the judge to consider. Sometimes probation staff will conduct psychological or other evaluations in order to help understand the needs of the youth. Recommendations could include counseling, weekend confinement in a secure facility, and/or restitution. These conditions become part of the youth's formal probation, and if the youth successfully completes the conditions, the case is terminated. About 60 percent of adjudicated delinquents are referred to this kind of formal probation.

The court may order the youth to be committed to some type of residential facility. These may be publicly or privately operated, and could be a secure (locked) facility or a more open group home, ranch, or camp type of environment. In some places the judge decides where the youth is placed; in others, the juvenile probation staff decides. The term of commitment could be for a stated period, or it could be open ended. Review hearings are held periodically to monitor the youth's progress in the facility. Access to psychological counseling, substance abuse treatment, or sex abuse treatment may or may not be provided.

After the youth is released, the court usually orders a period of aftercare, similar to adult parole, where the youth is under the supervision of the court or corrections staff. The youth is required to satisfy specific conditions of release, such as observing a curfew, attending school, and going to counseling, and if he or she does not satisfy those conditions, the youth could be recommitted to the facility.

TYPES OF FACILITIES

Several different types of facilities house juvenile offenders: secure detention, secure corrections, open (also known as "staff-secure") ranches or camps, and group homes. The purpose of secure detention in general is to hold pre-adjudicated or accused juveniles who, in the view of the probation officer, might pose a danger to themselves or others, or who might tend to not show up at their hearing. Youth are usually housed in units according to a number of factors such as sex, age, risk factor, or gang affiliation. Youth who have been adjudicated may also be held in secure detention to serve their sentence as well.

Thus a detention center may be used as a short-term holding place for youth waiting a few hours or days for a detention hearing or waiting a few weeks for adjudication, and/or be used for longer term stays of several months or more for post-adjudication detention or treatment. Detention centers are often administered locally by a county, municipality, or juvenile court.

A juvenile *corrections* facility houses youth who have committed serious crimes and are serving out sentences of a year or longer. Depending on state law, some of these youth might be transferred to adult prison when they reach 18, 19, or some other designated age. Correctional facilities are often state run.

Ranches and camps house youth for terms usually ranging from 6–9 months to a year or more. These facilities might be secure (locked) or open. Group homes might be used as a step in the reentry process, and a youth's stay there might depend on his or her completion of some requirement such as a substance abuse treatment program of weeks or months. Many ranches and camps are privately run.

Length of stay and level of security have definite implications for the kinds of services libraries can offer, the kinds of programming that might be offered, and how the librarian will be able to interact with youth. Youth who are detained for only a short time awaiting adjudication may not be present in the facility long enough to participate fully in library activities such as book discussion or other programs, or may not have library time on their schedules. Group homes or remote camps or ranches may not have library facilities onsite, and may not have staff available to bring youth to the facilities where the library is located.

3

Information Needs of Youth in Detention

I don't know what I would do without the library; I think I would go crazy without having something to read.

—17-year-old resident at a detention facility

WHO ARE YOUR USERS? DEMOGRAPHICS OF YOUTH IN DETENTION TODAY

While it seems a relatively straightforward task to count and categorize the individuals in the juvenile justice system, it is actually complicated by several factors. First, annual admissions and release data do not reflect the daily residential population on any given day, which varies widely as youth can enter and exit the system fairly quickly. Several different sources of information collected at different times are therefore used to characterize juvenile populations in detention in this chapter.

The Census of Juveniles in Residential Placement (CJRP) is administered biennially by the U.S. Bureau of the Census, and provides data on youth in detention on a specified date. In general, youth are included if they meet certain criteria: under age 21, assigned a bed in a residential facility on census day, charged with an offense or court-adjudicated for an offense, and in residential placement because of that offense. In addition, in some states or localities, youths in detention are also held for non-delinquent status offenses (such as truancy), and others are detained because of neglect, abuse, or mental health referrals. These individuals are included in the CJRP. In 2006, approximately 93,000 juvenile offenders were held in residential facilities on census day; about another 10,000 were held pending adjudication. The CJRP does not include youths held in adult prisons or jails. Approximately 4,100 juveniles were held in adult prisons or jails in 1999. Table 3.1 lists the number of juveniles in residential placement on census day in 2006, including committed, detained, and diverted youth, not including juveniles held in adult facilities. Other complicating factors include the state-to-state variations in minimum

Table 3.1

Youth in residential placement, 2006

Location of offense	Number of residents
United States	92,854
Alabama	1,752
Alaska	363
Arizona	1,737
Arkansas	813
California	15,240
Colorado	2,034
Connecticut	498
Delaware	303
District of Columbia	339
Florida	7,302
Georgia	2,631
Hawaii	123
Idaho	522
Illinois	2,631
Indiana	2,616
Iowa	1,062
Kansas	1,053
Kentucky	1,242
Louisiana	1,200
Maine	210
Maryland	1,104
Massachusetts	1,164
Michigan	2,760
Minnesota	1,623
Mississippi	444
Missouri	1,293
Montana	243
Nebraska	735
Nevada	885
New Hampshire	189
New Jersey	1,704
New Mexico	471
New York	4,197
North Carolina	1,029
North Dakota	240
Ohio	4,149
Oklahoma	924
Oregon	1,254
Pennsylvania	4,323
Rhode Island	348
South Carolina	1,320
South Dakota	597
Tennessee	1,419
Texas	8,247
Utah	864
Vermont	54

(continued)

Location of offense	Number of residents
Virginia	2,310
Washington	1,455
West Virginia	579
Wisconsin	1,347
Wyoming	315
Tribal facilities	132
Not reported	1,467

Source: "Residential Placement by State." In *Census of Juveniles in Residential Placement Databook, 2006*. Washington, DC: Office of Juvenile Justice and Delinquency Prevention (OJJDP). http://www.ojjdp.gov/ojstatbb/cjrp/

and maximum ages of youths held, as well as variations in types of offenses. The following information provides a generalized view of demographic characteristics nationwide.

AGE OF JUVENILES IN DETENTION

Youths in detention range in age from under 12 to over 21. The majority of youth in detention in 2006 were between 15 and 17 years old, and the majority of youth in detention were male. About 7,600 youth under age 18 were held in adult jails (not included in Figure 3.1).

Figure 3.1

Age and sex of youths in residential placement, 2006

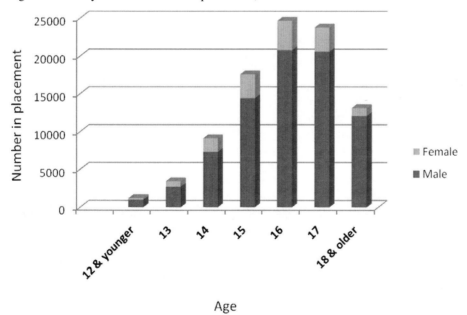

Source: Author's analysis of "Age on Census Day by Sex for United States, 2006." In *Census of Juveniles in Residential Placement Databook, 2006*. Washington, DC: Office of Juvenile Justice and Delinquency Prevention (OJJDP). http://www.ojjdp.gov/ojstatbb/cjrp/

Figure 3.2
Residents by race/ethnicity, 2006

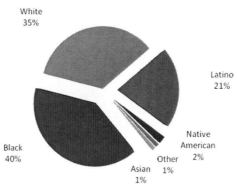

Source: Author's analysis of "Age on Census Date by Race/Ethnicity for United States, 2006." In *Census of Juveniles in Residential Placement Databook, 2006*. Washington, DC: Office of Juvenile Justice and Delinquency Prevention (OJJDP). http://www.ojjdp.gov/ojstatbb/cjrp/

RACE AND ETHNICITY

Nationally, black and Hispanic youth together make up over half of the incarcerated population. White youth make up a little more than a third; Asian, Native American, and others account for the remaining 4 percent (see Figure 3.2).

STATUS OFFENDERS VERSUS DELINQUENT OFFENDERS

As mentioned earlier, there are two different kinds of trouble a youth can get into in the eyes of the juvenile justice system. A *delinquent offense* is an act that, if committed by an adult, would be considered criminal. A *status offense* is behavior that is not criminal by adult standards but is not permitted for juveniles, such as running away, truancy, incorrigibility, and underage drinking. How these different types of offenses are viewed and handled varies from state to state. In some places, status offenses are considered violations of the law and are processed in the same manner as delinquent offenses. In others, status offenders are considered to be more in need of supervision rather than correction, and are referred to child welfare or other social services. Juveniles held for delinquent offenses accounted for 95 percent of all residents. Nationwide, status offenders accounted for 5 percent. Once again, this varies by state; in New York, for example, more than half of the youths entering residential detention facilities in 2007 were sent there for the equivalent of misdemeanor offenses, including truancy (Confessore 2009). (See Figure 3.3.)

CUSTODY RATE

The custody rate is the number of juveniles in residential placement per 100,000 juveniles ages 10 through the upper age of court jurisdiction in each state. In 1999 (the most recent year for which data are available), custody rates ranged from 96 youth incarcerated for every 100,000 youth in Vermont and Hawaii to 704 per 100,000 in the

Figure 3.3
Offenses by type, 2006

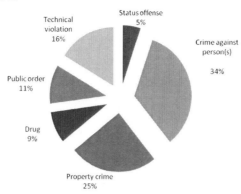

Source: Author's analysis of "Detailed Offense Profile for United States, 2006." In *Census of Juveniles in Residential Placement Databook, 2006*. Washington, DC: Office of Juvenile Justice and Delinquency Prevention (OJJDP). http://www.ojjdp.gov/ojstatbb/cjrp/

District of Columbia. Table 3.2 lists the state custody rates by upper age limit and state (Office of Juvenile Justice and Delinquency Prevention 2008). Figure 3.4 shows the overall custody rates in the United States by race or ethnicity: black teens were held in custody at five times the rate of white youth, at 1,004 black youth per 100,000 youth versus 212 white youth.

Table 3.2
Custody rate by state, 1999

State	Rate
Alabama	208
Alaska	281
Arizona	234
Arkansas	139
California	269
Colorado	257
Connecticut	160
Delaware	203
District of Columbia	173
Florida	306
Georgia	273
Hawaii	39
Idaho	203
Illinois	152
Indiana	280
Iowa	240
Kansas	239
Kentucky	192
Louisiana	223

(continued)

Table 3.2 (*continued*)

State	Rate
Maine	166
Maryland	136
Massachusetts	93
Michigan	243
Minnesota	183
Mississippi	118
Missouri	146
Montana	148
Nebraska	220
Nevada	305
New Hampshire	150
New Jersey	70
New Mexico	211
New York	169
North Carolina	123
North Dakota	204
Ohio	221
Oklahoma	194
Oregon	353
Pennsylvania	123
Rhode Island	155
South Carolina	244
South Dakota	436
Tennessee	170
Texas	204
Utah	267
Vermont	93
Virginia	225
Washington	232
West Virginia	166
Wisconsin	164
Wyoming	396

Source: Sickmund, Melissa. 2004. *Juveniles in Corrections.*
Washington, DC: Office of Juvenile Justice and Delinquency Prevention.

MENTAL HEALTH, SUBSTANCE ABUSE, AND OTHER ISSUES

Other characteristics of youth in detention indicate a very different kind of population than the school-age population outside of the justice system, particularly regarding disabilities, mental health, and substance abuse. About a third of youth in detention have some kind of disability, including learning disabilities, in contrast to 8 percent of youth outside. Ninety percent of incarcerated children meet diagnostic criteria for one or more mental health disorders, compared to 15 percent of high schoolers outside (Rozalski, Deignan, and Engel 2008). Special education services were also provided in 92 percent of juvenile corrections facilities (Freivalds 1996). In a sample of juvenile offenders released from Rikers Island,

Figure 3.4
Custody rate by race/ethnicity, 1999

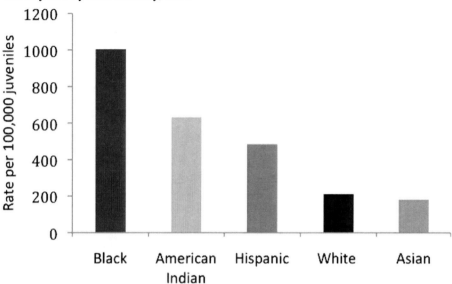

Source: Sickmund, Melissa. 2004. *Juveniles in Corrections*. Washington, DC: Office of Juvenile Justice and Delinquency Prevention.

New York, 64 percent reported a history of substance abuse issues (Landsberg and Rees 2009). Most detained youth meet criteria for a disruptive behavior disorder such as attention deficit hyperactivity disorder (ADHD) (Feldstein and Ginsburg 2009).

Not surprisingly, many of these youth also have emotional difficulties stemming from neglect, abuse, or chronic trauma, all of this in addition to being developing adolescents going through the emotional turmoil of that stage. Some youth are involved with the justice system for several years, perhaps coming in at 13 or 14 years old or younger, and getting out at age 18 to 24, a good portion of their lives. Many have not had the benefit of positive adult role models and have not learned basic commonsense rules of how to live in the world. Some youth released at age 18 may not have family support on the outside, yet they will still need to learn how to find a place to live, where to get counseling services and treatment, and a host of other tasks. How does a library meet the information needs of this group? More importantly, what are the information needs of this group?

INFORMATION NEEDS OF TEENS

Teens in general have an unfortunate reputation for distracting, if not outright disruptive, behavior in libraries. Patrick Jones notes that librarians who serve teens have a unique mission in helping guide young people on the path through adolescence (Jones 2007). Librarians for this group should share the belief that "reading, libraries, and lifelong learning can be positive forces in the lives of young people . . . [and] that young people will grow up to be caring and competent adults" (Jones 2007: 49). But in order to do this, the needs of these teens have to be at the center of our thinking. Too often, it has seemed easier to bar teens from the library to fix a behavior or noise problem rather than provide an environment that accommodates teens, let alone addresses the root causes of bad behavior.

Most children and adolescents experience some difficulties growing up. These are often manifested in some level of emotional upheaval, behavioral disorders, and/or learning problems (Travers 1982). Most of these problems dissipate as children grow up; some problems require more external support from parents, teachers, or others. Stress is a "daily universal reality" that children cope with mainly by simply enduring without assistance (Sorensen 1993). According to Doll, 20 percent of elementary school children meet the diagnostic criteria for one or more mental illnesses, and 80 percent of those children experience high levels of anxiety (Doll and Doll 1997). Similarly, 20 percent of high school students have a slight to serious psychiatric disorder, and a majority of that group is considered likely to consider or attempt suicide.

Librarians have been working harder to improve their understanding of teens in recent years, perhaps in response to studies indicating sizeable gaps between librarian perceptions of youth services and what teens actually experience and prefer in the library. A dozen years ago, the Public Libraries as Partners in Youth Development Initiative supported by the Urban Libraries Council concluded that teens had a very low opinion of public libraries, deeming them "uncool" and unwelcoming, with too many rules, unfriendly librarians, dreary spaces, and not enough technology (Meyers 1999). Other studies gathered similar negative opinions of teens on libraries. More than a few major library systems have since begun investing in creating comfortable and inviting teen spaces, enhancing information collections with more digital resources and new genres such as graphic novels, and developing programming specifically for young adults such as online games and social networking.

Recent research on the information needs of young adults has uncovered further aspects of teen information use and behavior that had previously gone unexplored. Denise Agosto led a study exploring the reasons why urban teens visit the library, and found that teens regarded the library not only as an information gateway to support schoolwork but also as a place for social interaction and entertainment, as a refuge to get away from a difficult home life or unsafe street environments, and as a place for personal learning and financial support (Agosto 2007). Cook, Parker, and Pettijohn also found that younger teens reported visiting the library for more than just doing research for school; they went to check out books for recreational reading, enjoy the café, attend activities with friends, and use the computers (Cook, Parker, and Pettijohn 2005).

Understanding what teens value about the library as a physical place does not cover all their information needs, however. In exploring how teens' information-seeking behavior functioned in everyday life, Hughes-Hassell and Agosto developed a model of teen development based on their everyday information needs (Hughes-Hassell and Agosto 2006). Information-seeking behavior was found to support seven areas of teen self-development: social, emotional, self-reflective, physical, creative, cognitive, and sexual development (see sidebar and Figure 3.5).

Figure 3.5
Information needs of teens

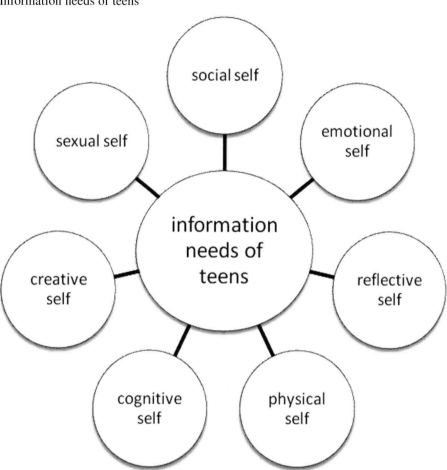

Source: Adapted from Hughes-Hassell and Agosto (2006).

EVERYDAY INFORMATION NEEDS OF TEENS

Information seeking related to *social development* refers to questions surrounding patterns of social behavior and cultural norms, particularly developing stable and productive peer relationships and understanding how to negotiate the social world.

Examples: What to do about fighting with friends, boy problems, what to wear at social functions, and how to act

Information needs related to *emotional development and self-reflection* refer to questions that teens ask as they work to establish internal emotional and psychological independence from parents, build a sense of identity and personal beliefs about the world, and develop impulse control and behavioral maturity. These information needs also help teens develop emotional health and help establish relationships with adults other than parents. Internal reflection helps teens develop a personal value system, a sense of civic duty, and vocational goals.

Examples: How to control anger, worrying about a family member or friend's safety, how to feel better after emotional upset, and wondering why people get sick and die.

Information needs related to the *physical self* deal with issues of safety and security, and of coping with the mundane issues of self-sufficiency in the external world, such as shopping for food, using public transportation, and paying bills.

Examples: How do I cook dinner, how can I get home safely, and how can I help my sibling with homework?

Information seeking of the *creative self* refers to the realization of aesthetic needs and artistic expression, such as questions about listening to music, watching a performance, or creating a work of art.

Examples: How can I learn how to make a demo of this song? Where can I find a DVD of that play?

Information seeking related to the *cognitive self* is concerned with the development of intellectual processing abilities and verbal skills, and the ability to respond to increased cognitive demands both academically in the school environment and in terms of understanding current events in the world.

Example: Researching and writing a term paper for school

Information seeking of the *sexual self* refers to comprehending the development of personal sexuality and sexual identity, and learning to recognize, accept, and manage one's sexuality.

Examples: Worrying about contracting a sexually transmitted disease, and questions about sexuality and bisexuality

Source: Adapted from Hughes-Hassell and Agosto (2006).

Ya Ling Lu noted that the information needs of children and teens were closely connected to their developmental stages, and that the information they seek is "essential to their growth in all aspects" (Lu 2005). Children's information queries often were pertinent to understanding their daily life activities and problems at home and at school, and were important for helping them develop empathy and coping skills.

Hughes-Hassell and Agosto recommend that librarians should go beyond providing homework help, recreational reading, and collections that support teen's developmental needs. Staff should be educated about the role of the library in supporting teen self-development, and teens should be involved in planning services and collections. Libraries should work with community partners to figure out ways of supporting teen development, including adults such as ministers, physicians, and counselors who can serve as mentors. Librarians should establish relationships with teens and families to "become part of the teens' network of trusted adults."

This way of thinking about the information needs of youth clearly goes beyond seeing the collection as merely supporting recreational reading, academic learning, and vocational preparation, and places librarians in a direct role as advisors and mentors who can help clarify the problems and issues that teens struggle with. Because teen information seeking and information needs are directly connected to their natural exploration of self and the world, library collections and services should be developed to address these needs, and librarians should know how to engage teens in the library.

COGNITIVE AND BEHAVIORAL ISSUES ASSOCIATED WITH JUVENILE DELINQUENCY

Youth who engage in delinquent activities have other issues that complicate their information needs. Poverty, abuse, and neglect are common. Many come from homes where the adults do not read, and where reading is not encouraged. In this kind of environment with few "reading role models," it is very difficult for youth to develop good reading skills. They often have had a tough time in school, and many drop out before finishing high school. Their "world knowledge" is limited; some may never have traveled beyond their own neighborhoods.

Research on the developmental characteristics of the normal adolescent brain indicates that the brain continues to mature into the early to mid-twenties (msnbc.com 2007). Teens at ages 16 and 17 are more likely to act impulsively and less likely to consider the long-term consequences of their actions. They are more susceptible to peer pressure, and can be more emotionally volatile and aggressive. As youths grow up and mature during their twenties, these characteristics tend to fade as they develop better judgment, self-control, and self-awareness. Studies on brain development have found physical changes in brain functioning that parallel this behavioral development.

Research in developmental psychology has shown that juvenile offenders display even more of these cognitive, behavioral, and emotional skill deficits, particularly consequential thinking and empathy. Juvenile offenders are thus even less likely to be able to consider the results of their actions and how their actions affect others (Guerra, Kim, and Boxer 2008). Compounding these developmental issues is the prevalence of substance abuse, mental illness, and other problems stemming from domestic abuse, neglect, and/or exposure to violence or other trauma.

Delinquent offenders often have an inflated, unrealistic sense of their own ego, and actually perceive situations differently than other (noncriminal) youth (e.g., "It's not my fault," or "He made me mad so I hit him [or stole or damaged something, etc.]"). These teens have perhaps even less adequate critical-reasoning, decision-making, and problem-solving abilities than their non-delinquent peers.

Although these challenges are formidable, positive cognitive behaviors and skills can be taught, and offenders who have success in learning and practicing these skills are less likely to continue to commit crimes (Alford and Larson 1987). It follows, then, that juveniles in detention would benefit from library collections, services, and programs that support in some way the development of consequential thinking, empathy, and other cognitive, social, and behavioral skills (Blinn 1995). The following chapter introduces current approaches to these services and programs for juveniles in detention.

4

Information Services for Youth
in Detention

On the surface, core information services in the juvenile detention center libraries in this study look quite a bit like those found in the teen section of a typical public library or middle or high school library center. Access to appropriate materials in the collection, reader's advisory, information and computer literacy instruction, and programming are all considered core services in most libraries that serve this age group. Programming in the form of book discussion is particularly important. Other factors also influence the types of information services offered to youth in detention, such as their specialized information needs and emerging trends in juvenile justice. In response to better understanding of these influences, library services in many facilities are expanding their focus beyond recreational reading and literacy.

THE TREND TOWARD BALANCED AND RESTORATIVE JUSTICE

A lot more is known now about the cognitive and behavioral characteristics of young offenders, and this has influenced a shift in the way youth in the criminal justice system are treated, moving away from punishment and medical or psychological treatment models to a "balanced and restorative" approach (Freivalds 1996). The restorative justice model is an important emerging perspective that is improving how the justice system prepares youth to be constructive, positive members of society.

Restorative justice focuses on three tenets: accountability, community, and competency development. Youth need to become accountable for their actions, the community needs to be involved with helping youth succeed, and youth need to develop the positive social skills and intellectual capacity to be productive members of society. This model has the potential to influence the development of more effective library services, as Isaac Gilman points out:

By expanding the vision of detention library services to reach beyond literacy and recreational reading, libraries can become integral partners in the mission of the juvenile courts—affecting a positive change in teens and their communities. (Gilman 2008)

The restorative justice approach requires an intensive support system throughout the justice system and community to ensure that there are means by which youth can be directly encouraged to develop positive social attitudes and behaviors. Libraries can support and promote restorative justice principles in countless ways through focused reader's advisory, collection development, and programs. From the start, librarians need to focus on how they interact with youth: every contact, every conversation, and every book checkout is an opportunity to teach, model, and demonstrate pro-social behavior and good decision making. This is no different from good practice in teen services on the outside; librarians should have high expectations for good behavior, and actively encourage positive social interaction (Walter and Meyers 2003). It is no different in detention.

Second, collections should be developed to include fiction that resonates with this group of youth, and broadens minds and attitudes, and wide-ranging nonfiction to introduce new knowledge to teens across disciplines. Stories that portray familiar environments and challenges will resonate. School library collections in detention should support and enrich the education program. Collections should certainly support programming that focuses on restorative principles. Finally, the collection should be a base of resources for staff as well. Facility librarians can work with public and school libraries in the youths' home communities to support access to resources for youth, families, and others in the community on reentry. Chapter 7 offers specific guidance on collection development in detention libraries.

Library instruction and other programs can be developed to specifically target and promote the development of consequential thinking, empathy, and other pro-social and positive cognitive skills. Readings and book discussions can focus on stories that involve characters and situations that demonstrate consequential thinking and empathy. Model programs explored for this study are described in detail in Chapter 6.

Collections and programming are the basic elements of information services in detention; however, the interactions that librarians have with youth through reader's advisory is where librarians can have a potent impact with youth. Modeling and encouraging positive behavior are important, but librarians should also focus on meeting these teens' special information needs, which can be complex and challenging. Youth need guidance to help them get the most from the library to meet these goals.

A SPECIAL KIND OF READER'S ADVISORY

A 2008 survey indicated that 80 percent of detention librarians believed that their most important function was to provide access to "recreational reading to pass time" and to promote literacy (Gilman 2008). Gilman argues that these functions alone do not adequately serve the information needs of detained juveniles with their mixed bag of cognitive, emotional, and behavioral problems. Similarly, the librarians in the present study were of two minds in terms of how they perceived their roles and functions in serving youth. Some librarians felt that they should focus on providing information, facilitating access, and instructing youth while steering somewhat clear of closer engagement: "If you want to be a social worker or a counselor of some kind, being a librarian in here is not going to be satisfying. That's just not going to work."

At the same time, however, librarians were in agreement that their top priorities were to get youth interested in reading, increase their literacy, and *use reading to help them overcome their problems*. Many agreed that the best way to help youth do these things was to connect closely with their interests, issues, and problems; tailor reading recommendations to those needs; and talk to the teens about what they are reading. Librarians generally felt that the best service on this level involved engagement with youth well beyond the superficial information need, by getting to know them, establishing trust, and developing relationships: "It's important to take the extra step of talking to the kids about what they are reading. Ideally you should ask them, 'Tell me what you're thinking.'"

When it comes to recommending books to read and talking to teens about what they were reading, however, some of the conflict for librarians seemed to come from different places: determining which reading material was right for the individual versus determining what kind of engagement was appropriate. How deeply do we need to understand a teen's interests and needs in order to best serve him or her? The basic assumption of reader's advisory, after all, is that it is possible for a librarian to be able to recommend good materials to a youth, based on knowledge of the youth's interests and needs (Sturm 2003). It is clear that the better librarians understand the specialized needs of the teens in their libraries, the better served the youth will be.

Beyond suggesting interesting books, however, it is important to recognize the unique functions and benefits of reading for these youth. Reading has definite therapeutic value for individuals with psychological or emotional problems, even when individuals are given books to read with minimal guidance (Renwick 2009). Children and teens in particular benefit from reading in many ways: reading decreases their sense of isolation, reduces depression, and helps validate thoughts and emotions. Reading helps children gain insight into personal problems, and helps them develop empathy (Berns 2004). Reading stories has also been shown to be an effective strategy to help youth manage difficult problems and get a handle on complex thoughts and feelings that are difficult to understand (Pehrsson and McMillen 2005).

Achieving these benefits from reading does not happen in a vacuum, however. The librarians in this study specifically emphasized how they helped youth with decision making, critical thinking, and problem solving through their everyday interactions and reading recommendations. The interaction is vital; it is not enough to merely put the books out on the shelves, or even to put a book in a teen's hands:

If you limit yourself to only providing a 'book of the month club,' you are missing out on a big part of what you could be doing. You have to instruct, do some kind of cognitive teaching to help them learn how to think.

COGNITIVE-BEHAVIORAL THERAPY

Cognitive-behavioral therapy (CBT) is the formal psychological term for a number of "talk-therapy" or discussion protocols that help individuals identify problems, become aware of personal thoughts and beliefs about situations, and identify negative or inaccurate thinking. The goal is to use this understanding to discover alternative, positive ways of thinking and change negative behavior. CBT has been shown to strengthen the development of consequential thinking and increase positive behaviors of juveniles in detention (Bennion 1986). Some detention facilities provide training to staff in basic CBT principles (Dittman 2007).

Many of the most effective book discussion programs for youth in detention make use of CBT-like discussion routines. *Character-based literacy* is a type of literary analysis that uses stories to explore characters' choices and thought processes. Youth apply the experiences of characters in stories to their own lives to help them recognize and adjust their own negative choices or behavior patterns. Book discussion programs like these have been used frequently and successfully with children in treatment for emotional difficulties, particularly in combination with creative expression through writing, music, or art.

Encouraging constructive problem solving, decision making, and self-awareness by discussing stories is a vital service that librarians can provide in detention facilities. Chapter 6 presents descriptions of many of these model programs.

CHARACTER-BASED LITERACY

Angier and O'Dell outlined some general discussion questions that can be adapted for character-based book discussion with juveniles in detention. Here are some highlights:

- What did you like about this story? What didn't you like?
- What do you think the author was trying to do by telling this story?
- Has anything like what happened in this story ever happened to you or someone you know?
- What do you think about the main character? How do you feel about his [or her] actions?
- What was the most important scene?
- How is your neighborhood [or school, family, etc.] the same or different from the one in this story?

Source: Adapted from Angier, Naomi, and Katie O'Dell. 2000. The book group behind bars. *Voice of Youth Advocates* 23 (5): 331–333.

ENGAGEMENT: BUILDING RELATIONSHIPS AND TRUST WITH YOUTH

In addition to their knowledge of the materials to suggest, public service librarians also define their competence in terms of the way they interact with users, including their ability to communicate with users and discern users' needs. This is another vital level to the relationship that librarians share with juveniles in detention and the roles that they play in those relationships. Closer relationships with users have been associated with expertise in studies of the skill level of teachers, nurses, and counselors (Benner 1982), as well as expertise in library reference work, including reader's advisory (Sweeney 2008). Once again, the better the librarians know the teen, the better they can help. This was obvious with the juvenile detention librarians in this study:

It would be ideal to see the same teens over and over and actually form relationships. . . . The ones I know the best were here for six to eight months; I got to know them and their families. But others are only here for a short while so we only see them once or twice.

Librarians observed the need to spend time to build trust with youth. These are teens who have not necessarily had good adult role models during adolescence, or even in some cases throughout childhood. By virtue of their recent interactions with law enforcement, they are suspicious of authority in general and the adults "in the system" in particular. And they may be scared to death of where they find themselves at the present moment. No matter how hardened they may seem on the surface, underneath they are still teens growing up. They need to experience positive interactions with adults, and they need to learn how to build trust. Another librarian described how she valued the time she spent getting to know the youth and building trust:

I try to spend most afternoons with the kids, delivering books that they've requested, things that I think they will like. I'm just sitting and spending time with them, visiting with them either in groups or one on one. Just to talk with them about books, try to connect with them, just be a positive person. . . . My role is to say "Who are you and what would you like to read?"

At the same time, there will be times when issues come up that are out of the librarian's realm of responsibility or knowledge, such as when a youth brings up a serious personal problem. It is important to be able to refer the youth to a social worker or other counselor, or at least make sure counselors know that the issue came up: "It's amazing what literature can do to bring out some of these things that don't come out in the assessment interviews [with the social workers]."

It's hard to explain the work that we do. It's really about building a relationship with the youth. You want them to like you but you have to have boundaries. Same with the staff.

FREE VOLUNTARY READING (OR, HOW DETENTION LIBRARIES BOOST LITERACY)

Clearly something more begins to happen in these librarian-youth interactions as the teens discover the potential of books to help them learn in ways that were not previously accessible to them:

What's really cool about the library is that they come in and say "I want something that will help me expand my mind" and "I want to read something that's about more than my block." He knows enough to know that [his block] is a very small part of the world and he is asking me for something that's more than that.

Librarians can help youth learn that they can read for pleasure as well as for education, and that they can take charge of what they are reading and what they are learning. For many, this is a new experience. "Education" in many of their minds has always been something that was forced upon them, yet another aspect of their lives that they cannot control. Education and school are often associated with negative experiences for these youths. The fact that librarians can help teens move beyond these negative associations is an extraordinary accomplishment, and should be a fundamental goal of teen services in detention:

That's my role: to help them see reading as for pleasure or for education or both. They can take charge of that part of their life. It's also about information literacy, trying to get the kids to understand how to get information for themselves. For the most part these kids are not information literate at all.

This group of young people is different from their non-incarcerated peers in many ways, particularly in terms of their reading skill level and attitudes toward reading. Juveniles tend to come into the corrections system with lower literacy skills than their peers on the outside, and generally have had negative experiences with reading. Many have already stopped attending school. Estimates of reading levels at entry range from three to five years below grade level; OJJDP estimates the average reading ability of youth in corrections at the fourth-grade level (Hodges, Giuliotti, and Porpotage 1994).

The fact that these youth come into the system with low reading skill and a tough attitude does not mean that they are destined to remain poor readers, however. Although this project gathered only anecdotal evidence on reading skill and literacy, there is a growing body of empirical research on how much progress youth make in reading while they are in detention. Education researchers have consistently connected reading improvement, instructional programs, and curriculum with increased literacy and reduced recidivism (Hodges, Giuliotti, and Porpotage 1994; Krezmien and Mulcahy 2008).

A principal of one detention center high school noted that students inside typically gain up to three grade levels after only a few months of reading while in residential programs. More than one librarian in this study remarked that teachers and principals in local public schools notice big changes in the reading levels of youth who return to school after a stay in detention: "they can tell the kids have been reading inside."

Stephen Krashen argues that people who read for pleasure naturally and inevitably improve their reading comprehension, enlarge their vocabulary, and improve grammar, spelling, and punctuation, and thus enable themselves to better handle the "complex literacy demands of modern society" (Krashen 2004). Encouraging youth to engage in what Krashen calls "free voluntary reading" is one of the most important things librarians can do, especially in detention. Being able to choose what they want to read is essential, as one librarian pointed out:

I firmly believe that choice is one of the most important functions of the library. The more I interact with these kids, the more I see they need to have the ability to choose. Their entire day is otherwise dictated.

Another librarian had a similar opinion:

The library media center in any school is a place where students should have free will. Students in detention have very little free will. We are trying to give them the opportunity to have one place where they can come and make a choice and have a positive result. Hopefully they will like the book they are reading and that will encourage them to read some more.

The library may well be one of the only places in the detention center where the youth can exercise meaningful choice. Most activities are directed and monitored: youth go where they are told, they eat when they are told, and they go to class when they are told. They are given clothes to wear and may not be permitted to have any personal property at all. In secure facilities, their every movement is watched and controlled. They may have to walk in a single file with their hands behind their backs to get from place to place.

These elements of control and structure are an important part of helping many teens gain control of their behavior, especially if they are coming from an environment that has provided poor guidance thus far. However, Veysey points out that youth in trouble also need to be empowered to be involved in their treatment and to take ownership of their own growth and development (Veysey 2008). In the library setting, letting the teen choose what he or she wants to read is an opportunity for taking ownership, gaining confidence in exercising decision making, and exploring new areas of knowledge.

This is not to suggest that what youth do in the detention library is not monitored. Unlike in school, where students are assigned reading, in the libraries in this study the teens were not told what they should read. Youth were free to pick up whatever they were interested in, no questions asked. As Krashen puts it, they are reading because they want to. There are no tests, no notes, and no book reports. Krashen tells us that while this type of reading does not necessarily produce high levels of competency very quickly (earlier anecdotal evidence aside), it provides the foundation upon which that competency can be built. It allows youth to explore their own emerging interests on their own.

The library as a place of freedom of choice and safety in choice is critical for nurturing a liking for reading. If the library is a place where you don't get laughed at for wanting to read a comic book, where the librarian seems to genuinely like you and wants to help you find what you want, and where you are shown respect for your choices, you will want to return. You will have good feelings about reading, something that many of these youth may not have experienced before.

GETTING THEM STARTED: CREATING A CULTURE OF READING

How do teens who supposedly "can't read" and who often have had miserable experiences in school become readers? In some respects, youth inside are a captive audience: it does not take long for residents to realize that outside of required class time, mealtime, and scattered appointments and activities, there is not a lot to do in detention. They could have a lot of "room time," that is, time spent alone in their individual rooms. As it is on the outside, boredom is a huge problem for teens, and reading can help them pass the time at the very least. Librarians in detention can help residents find something they are interested in to read, the basic function of reader's advisory.

Some will head straight for the comic books and graphic novels, others to teen and young adult fiction, and others to all the other corners of the collection. Arguably, there is very little teens are not interested in, although there are the same fads and surges of interest in detention as in libraries everywhere. The librarian has to be nonjudgmental; preteens may just want to look at *Where's Waldo* and escape from the world for an hour. Another will want to know, "Where's that stuff that goes with killin' and cussin'?" Appropriateness and other issues in collection development policies are addressed later in Chapter 7.

It is the librarian's job to understand and validate the individual's choice (even if that choice cannot be fulfilled, there are always alternatives, and that is part of the challenge). This is critical trust-building: the residents need to realize that they are not going to be laughed at for their choices, and that librarians will in fact go out of their way to spend time helping them find something interesting to read. For many of these youth, no one has ever done this for them before. This can be a life-changing concept:

The kids are used to people making fun of them for wanting those [comic books or *Where's Waldo*]. . . . As soon as they come in and I give them those things and take them seriously, they start to realize that I am taking them seriously and they become respectful. They look around for other people who will be that way with them.

"THE FIRST TIME I READ A BOOK IT WAS IN HERE"

I asked one librarian, "How many kids really get into reading while they are here?" "All of them," she shot back emphatically. "Well, maybe one or two won't read. But once they start they don't stop." In the course of this study, I heard story after story of the reluctant-reader-turns-into-voracious-insatiable-reader. Another librarian told me about a resident who exemplified the rapid growth in reading skill shown by some residents. "José" (not his real name), age 17, had been in and out of juvenile hall since he was 14, and had developed a good relationship with the librarians over the years. He described how he really didn't read at all before he came into the center, "just for school and I never liked school much." When he first started reading in the detention center library, it was with a comic book. When he finished that, he asked for something else, anything really, and the librarian gave him some teen fiction. He came back again and again over the following weeks, asking for progressively more and more challenging materials.

He then discovered the nonfiction section, and began reading "anything I have a question about." He was working his way through the philosophy section at the time we talked, and was fascinated with "Plato and all that stuff."

Now age 17, Jose will be a father in a few months, like many teens in detention, and so he has been reading up on pregnancy and parenting. José has discovered how he can use the library to teach himself about the world: "I had no idea about all this stuff out in the world. All I knew before was my own block. . . . I'm using my time in here to educate myself."

What was truly remarkable is that the youth using the libraries in this study talked frequently to each other about what they were reading as naturally as breathing. Youth wanted to share the books they enjoyed, or did not enjoy, and there was plenty of book-related conversation among the residents. This enthusiasm often carried over into successful book clubs and discussion groups. A librarian explained what typically happened in her library:

A lot of the kids do reader's advisory with each other. It's really beautiful. I had them write recommendations to put next to the book but that didn't really take off. But the kids will say to each other, you need to read this book, kid. Now it happens all the time. If it's busy and a kid will ask me what to read, the kid next to him will say, what do you like? They have great questions, and they always have an idea if I'm stumped.

5

Detention Library Service Models

What kinds of library arrangements, programs, and services will you find in juvenile detention centers? The answer to that is: all kinds. The ways in which detention libraries and services are organized, presented, and utilized, and exactly what services and programs are actually offered, vary widely from place to place in this study. This section describes three common models of juvenile detention library organization and service demonstrated by the institutions studied for this project: the school library, the public library, and outreach. The libraries in the juvenile detention institutions in this study tended to serve dual school and public library purposes, blending aspects of school and public libraries in their organizations, approaches, and services. Staffing arrangements spanned the range of full-time professional public librarians, school librarians, trained library assistants, part-time outreach librarians, community volunteers, teachers, and clerical staff. Training for these individuals varied widely.

THE SCHOOL LIBRARY

The school library model was fairly common in the libraries in this study, often housed adjacent to or within classrooms, and run just like a typical school library in an ordinary public school. In some cases, the local school district was responsible for running the school as well as the library. These libraries were usually staffed by a certified school librarian, teacher, educational aide, or other school district employee reporting to the principal, or by detention staff.

Some facilities administer separate educational and library programs for long- and short-term youth. Other groups with special needs or who are being treated for specific offenses (such as sex offenders) might also be segregated from the general youth population. Educational programs for these different groups may be administered separately or together. Separate programs often mean different sets of teachers, curricula, and procedures.

Educational curriculum is often approached differently in the detention setting as compared to schools on the outside. With so many students rapidly cycling in and out of the system, students with radically different learning skills, and students with an array of emotional and behavioral issues, more time might be spent on behavior control than on learning. Classroom work might focus more on basic skill development in language arts and math while introducing historical, scientific, and other concepts. Because students may not be assigned homework to complete outside the detention classroom (often because they may not be permitted to have pens, pencils, or other materials outside the classroom), work must be completed during the class session. Despite these limitations, librarians can still present information literacy skill-building activities to support classroom learning.

Teachers, however, may have varying levels of understanding of the kinds of creative and productive information literacy activities that librarians can provide. Librarians should build relationships with teachers in order to work these activities into the classroom curriculum.

In the locations in this study, library visits were often coordinated with the school day schedule, with a period set aside for library, or with a teacher setting aside time for a class visit every week or two. Students might be sent to the library in groups for an entire period, sent from class singly or in pairs for brief visits, or sent occasionally as a "time out" for behavioral issues. Library instruction might be incorporated into regular classroom time or visits to the library. One librarian scheduled regular 30-minute instruction sessions on curriculum-relevant topics every time the classes visited the library. Instruction was followed by 15 minutes of book selection and checkout. Another librarian, whose library was not adjacent to the classrooms, brought books to the classrooms during certain periods and occasionally taught a library instruction session at the teacher's request. In some states, school librarians are required to hold a teaching certification as well as a library science certification, and are classified and paid as teachers, even in juvenile corrections.

PASSAGES ACADEMY LIBRARIES, NEW YORK

Passages Academy is a full-time educational program for residents in custody of the New York City Department of Juvenile Justice, a corrections system that takes in over 5,000 youth each year (New York City Department of Juvenile Justice 2007). Rebecca Howlett, a social studies teacher hired by Passages Academy in 1998, was shocked to discover that there were no libraries available to students "who were locked inside a building for twenty-four hours a day, seven days a week" (Fenster-Sparber 2008). Some books were located in the dormitory areas, but these tended to be limited to marked-up GED prep books, tattered Bibles, and perhaps a copy of *The Cross and the Switchblade* or *The Von Trapp Family Singers*. When she first brought books into her classroom, the students were overjoyed to have something to read.

Rebecca Howlett went on to forge relationships with corrections administrators, officers, and educators, paving the way for the institution's first library in 2003. Now expanded to seven sites, the libraries support recreational reading needs of the students and are starting to provide information literacy instruction.

The Passages Academy library team consists of two certified school librarians, two literacy teachers, a library coordinator, a library assistant, and an education paraprofessional. A close relationship with the Office of School Library Services in New York City provides guidance.

Collections have grown to several thousand books, circulation is increasing, and author events and special programs are popular. Technology upgrades and space renovations are next steps.

Facility rules do have an impact on library use: "Passages' students cannot move through the building without escorts. As a result, students do not visit the libraries independently. . . . Developing and maintaining positive relationships with the Department of Juvenile Justice staff who supervise students' safety is essential" (Fenster-Sparber 2008).

Contact: Jessica Fenster-Sparber, Library Coordinator

literacyforteens@aol.com

718-292-0065, ext. 219

http://web.me.com/palibraries

http://whatsgoodinthelibrary.blogspot.com

THE PUBLIC LIBRARY

In contrast to the school library, the library within the detention facility might be administered as a branch of the local public library, or as an outreach service through the public library. Books, materials, and the librarian's salary might come directly from the public library, and the librarian may report to the library's head of public or youth services, or perhaps an outreach or program coordinator. A deposit collection might be used to serve the facility.

Some libraries based on this model try hard to make their libraries true microcosms of public libraries outside, from using the Dewey system to having a computer catalog, databases, and reference resources, and providing continuing education resources and community referrals. Young adult services librarians in a detention library do the same things they do in public libraries outside: help youth find something interesting to read, introduce teens to the vastness of what they can get out of the library and what the library can do for them, and create and provide interesting programs.

The public library model fits well with the correction system's mission to prepare residents for reentry into society because of the public library's traditional focus on self-help, information competency, and lifelong learning. For the youth in the system, this can include help in developing basic academic and life skills that they may not have been taught or even exposed to before they were placed in the system. Youth also need to have access to GED preparation and other educational materials, vocational materials, and career-seeking guidance such as how to write a resume, how to apply for a job online, where to look for employment, and how to apply to community college.

SAN FRANCISCO PUBLIC LIBRARY AT JUVENILE JUSTICE CENTER

The San Francisco Public Library (SFPL) at Juvenile Justice Center (JJC) is a small branch library located within the school at the Juvenile Justice Center, staffed with a full-time professional librarian and one half-time page. Housed in a pleasant windowed space adjacent to the classrooms, library books and materials are arranged in shelves and displays along the outer walls, with a display rack or two in the center of the room with a table and seating for four to six people.

Youth are in school every weekday, and language arts teachers set aside one period a week for library use. Residents might be sent to the library a few at a time for 10 to 15 minutes, and the librarian is there to help them find what they want to read. Other teachers might send in a whole class for the whole period. The probation department does not make time for library visits outside of school time, so it is important that the teachers care enough to make library visits possible.

Youth in the maximum security unit are not currently permitted to come to the library, so the librarian brings a book truck to them every week in their units during their language arts class. The librarian brings books and magazines based on what she knows they are interested in, as well as materials they have requested.

The main collection at JJC is a stand-alone collection. Although it is part of the SFPL system, items are not represented in the main SFPL catalog, and the library does not place holds on materials elsewhere in the system. A computer catalog is available for the librarian's use; residents do not have access to it. Small deposit collections are housed in each of the living units; the librarian visits these periodically to refresh the collections.

Contact: San Francisco Public Library at Juvenile Justice Center, 375 Woodside Ave., San Francisco, CA 94127; 415-753-7845.

YOUTH SERVICE CENTER LIBRARY, KING COUNTY LIBRARY SYSTEM

The Youth Service Center is the juvenile hall for King County in Seattle, Washington, and its library is an institutional branch of the King County Library System. Situated in a good-sized interior space adjacent to the classrooms, the library has a large collection arrayed on shelves around the perimeter of the room as well as on low bookcases at one end of the room. Library tables with seating for 12 are in constant use for library instruction, tutoring, and reading. New books are scattered around for residents to peruse. "We found that if we displayed the books more formally, nobody touched them. If they are just on the tables scattered around, the kids will pick them up."

Nine computer workstations arranged along two walls have office software and Internet access, and are in constant use during residents' free periods. While they are not permitted to freely browse the Internet, they can visit a number of pre-approved sites. Music sites are very popular. All of the computer monitors are visible from the librarian's office and workspace, which is behind glass with an open window for checkout. A printer is available for the residents; teens often like to print out favorite song lyrics. Staff reviews the printouts for appropriateness. Residents who visit unauthorized Web sites lose their computer privileges for the duration of their stay.

Comfortable couches and low tables at the entrance to the room make this library a popular gathering place for service center staff, and there is a collection of professional materials for staff development. The entire holdings of the King County Library System is accessible to staff and residents through the online catalog.

The library is open seven days a week. All residents visit the library with their living unit groups twice a week with their supervising officer, once for a library instruction session and once for free time. Each living unit group has about 10 to 12 residents. On weekends, residents can visit the library during their free time.

Contact: Youth Service Center Library, 1211 East Alder, Seattle, WA 98122; 206-343-2641.

SECOND CHANCE BOOKS

Second Chance Books is an award-winning collaborative outreach effort of the Austin Public Library and the Gardner Betts Juvenile Justice Center. Started in 2003, Second Chance provides two satellite branches of the Austin Public Library with a combined collection of over 4,000 volumes for casual reading. These branches are housed at the short-term and long-term lockup facility of the Juvenile Justice Center. In addition to the two libraries on site, Second Chance offers book clubs, author visits, art programs, and special presentations for the young adults in these facilities.

Contact: Second Chance Books, Austin Public Library, P.O. Box 2287, Austin, TX 78768-2287; 512-974-9830; Kathleen Houlihan, Youth Program Librarian: Kathleen.Houlihan@ci.austin.tx.us.

LIVING UNIT COLLECTIONS

Whether the library is administered by the school district, a public library, volunteers, or detention staff, many facilities often have shelf space set aside for deposit collections in the living units. In some cases, these collections are the only library collections in the facility. While they might be minimal and not provide the quantity or variety of a stand-alone library, living unit collections provide access to reading materials while accommodating unpredictable activities such as lockdowns, transfers, and other situations typical in detention that can disrupt visits to the library. Youth can check out and return books to the living unit shelves without worrying about getting a book back to the library by a particular due date.

OUTREACH

In yet other facilities, the local public library, a state library agency, or a local non-profit organization might provide library services to the facility via an outreach program where library staff, volunteers, or others provide books, programming, and/or other services on a visiting basis. Some youth corrections facilities rely completely on volunteers to collect and deliver donated books. Many facilities do not have sufficient dedicated space for a separate library, so books might be stored on shelves in common areas, in closets, or in classrooms. In some facilities there is no space for book storage, and materials must be transported into and out of the facility at each visit.

Library outreach services can be as simple as delivering books to living units on a cart, or can include a range of library services such as reader's advisory, instruction, interlibrary loan, arts and crafts and other programs, and outside programming. The limits for outreach and volunteer services observed in this study seemed to be driven by a combination of factors such as what facility administrators will permit, the amount of time and resources available through the outside organization, and the energy and creativity of the library volunteer.

The outreach librarian may or may not have much contact with facility residents: in one facility, an outreach librarian from the local public library brings books from the public library to the facility where resident living unit leaders unload the books and take them to each unit. The librarian does not otherwise interact with any of the detention youth.

THE NIDORF COLLECTIVE, UCLA

During the 2004–2005 school year, the Young Adult and Children's Services student organization at UCLA's Department of Information Studies (YACS) began a student volunteer project at the Barry J. Nidorf Juvenile Detention Facility in Sylmar, in the north San Fernando Valley. Nidorf houses about 650 children and teens ages 12 to 17. Stays vary from as little as a few weeks to several years.

On discovering that there was no library or books available to residents at the facility, a group of students and librarians from the UCLA Information Studies graduate program created the Nidorf Collective, a group that solicits book donations from friends, family, libraries, and schools, and delivers them to the living units at Nidorf. During their weekly visits, they conduct book talking groups and give away books. UCLA students felt it was a perfect opportunity to reach teens who might never have read a book cover to cover before, to provide entertainment, and perhaps to provide them with books that could help them with their problems. The group also created the "Beyond 4 Walls Wish List" on Amazon.com to collect book donations (see http://www.amazon.com/gp/registry/3GB06L568M0Y3).

Contact: The Nidorf Collective: http://polaris.gseis.ucla.edu/yalsa/service.html

---

WATCH THESE

East Mesa Books: San Diego County Library:
http://www.youtube.com/watch?v=RUuobpgFTMg
Amy Cheney, Write to Read, Alameda County Library, Juvenile Hall Literacy:
http://video.google.com/videoplay?docid=-1897405466139718191#

Which is the best model of library service for youth in the corrections system? Each has advantages and disadvantages, and youth in detention can be well served or poorly served in any of these service models. Some librarians have deep-seated convictions about the best way to serve juveniles in detention:

At the time they asked me if I wanted to work for the school department. It was really a difficult decision. But I believe it's best for the library to be under the auspices of the public library. It makes your focus clear: free and voluntary reading. You want what the public library brings, the capacity for youth to have access to free reading. I absolutely support the school but my primary purpose is not curricular support—my primary purpose is free reading for the youth, which we know increases reading level.

The school librarians interviewed for this study all vigorously supported free voluntary reading and placed a high priority on bringing in materials that interested the students, and were sometimes able to advocate for controversial materials. This latter point, providing access to materials of real interest to students while maintaining a collection that administrators and teachers are comfortable with, is not as simple as it sounds in juvenile corrections, particularly in the school library environment. Collection development is discussed in Chapter 7.

OTHER SUPPORT FOR LIBRARY SERVICES: STATE INSTITUTIONAL LIBRARY CONSULTANTS

Some state library agencies employ consultants to assist institutional libraries associated with state-run facilities such as prisons, psychiatric hospitals, schools for the blind and deaf, and similar institutions. Consultants can be responsible for helping librarians and other service providers with training and technical support, collection maintenance and development, and funding. Consultants can be conduits of information on program ideas and grant opportunities, and may be able to provide other resources as well.

In some cases, the consultant may coordinate closely or work under contract with a state department of education or corrections, or with local public libraries or school districts. This type of coordinated support can be helpful for the many detention libraries that lack professional staffing. Library services in several of the juvenile detention centers in this project were provided by non-librarian volunteers, teachers, or administrative staff without library training.

A DAY IN A DETENTION LIBRARY

"We see the kids twice a week; library has its own period in the daily school schedule on Mondays through Fridays. Periods are 45 minutes long. One is a library class, and the other is free time. They come with their units, about 10 to 14 youths at a time. We have nine computer workstations, and for free time they are pretty much on the computers listening to music the whole time. For the library class, we do a library skills session on a database or a research topic, sometimes with a worksheet, and then they can check out their books. We work closely with the teachers here to plan our skills sessions. Saturday and Sunday the library is open for free time."

"The residents come in for 10 to 15 minutes and I help them find books as fast as I can. Then they go back to class and a new group comes in.. . . Sometimes I can get the whole class in the library for 45 minutes and that's much better. They get to browse and take their time looking for things. Even though there are lots of kids for me to juggle and try to help, it's much more fun. It really teaches them what a library can be like, how to browse and find your own books. When they are only in here for 10 minutes it's much more challenging. They don't really learn how the Dewey decimal system works or how to look for a book alphabetically. It's challenging."

TRENDS IN DETENTION FACILITY DESIGN AND CONSTRUCTION

New directions in juvenile detention administration are also influencing library services. The physical layouts of some new facilities combine living spaces with classrooms, kitchen facilities, and recreational areas in larger, self-contained spaces. This cuts down on the amount of youth movement within the facility, thus increasing security while simultaneously reducing the number of staff needed to supervise the youth. For facilities with stand-alone library spaces, it may become more of a challenge to make sure youth have adequate opportunities to experience the library. As these self-contained living spaces become more prevalent in new facilities, living unit collections may become more important in the future, and librarians may have to devise new ways of spending more time visiting youth in their units. Unfortunately, all too many new detention centers are still being designed without dedicated library space.

SECURITY POLICIES AFFECTING ACCESS TO LIBRARIES AND LIBRARY MATERIALS

In general, policies at the administrative level in a detention facility are minimally concerned with library services, if they mention the library at all. While audit standards from departments of youth services or education at the state or local levels may be in place, these are concerned with security, access to health services, and meeting educational content standards. Libraries are not mentioned in *Performance-Based Standards: Goals, Standards, Outcome Measures, Expected Practices and Processes*, the standards document from the Council of Juvenile Correctional Administrators, although there are several sections in which library services could be used to contribute to outcome measures, such as education, programming, and reintegration (Council of Juvenile Correctional Administrators 2010; see http://pbstandards.org/Default.aspx).

The Correctional Education Association (CEA) approved separate standards for accrediting juvenile correctional education programs in 2004, but these standards focus on meeting state educational program requirements such as classroom hours, special education, curriculum, and teacher certification. One standard addresses library services, although it is not a required standard (Correctional Education Association 2004) (see sidebar).

STANDARD # 44: LIBRARY SERVICES

"System wide policies and procedures and evidence of implementation and practice make Library Services accessible to students enrolled in the correctional education programs. The Library Services shall include:

- reference services
- education and vocational information and resources
- institution regulations and policies relevant to the population
- rehabilitative information (ex. drug abuse and addictive services)
- recreational reading
- reentry resources for job search skills, resume writing, etc.
- community information and resources
- a multitude of media to provide information (to include print materials, video and audio materials, computer software, etc., and necessary hardware)
- staffing to provide library services
- an annual budget provided from the institution or education budget for library services
- adequate space for the provision of library services."

Source: Correctional Education Association. 2004. *Performance Standards for Correctional Education Programs in Juvenile Institutions*. Elkridge, MD: Correctional Education Association.

Although this varies somewhat from place to place, the primary focus of virtually all policy statements in juvenile corrections is security and safety for residents and staff.

Library policies and procedures should reflect this focus and build upon it. Some facility policies may directly conflict with the library's intended services: some facilities do not permit hardcover books, DVDs, or Internet access. At least one facility in this study did not permit residents to carry anything, including books, while in transit from one part of the facility to another. This certainly presents a challenge to librarians who want youth to be able to have reading materials in their living spaces.

Librarians need to be creative in developing workarounds to security restrictions. Librarians in this study with the latter restriction took book orders from residents and delivered materials to their living units. Another facility did not permit youths to have books in their rooms, although loose paper was permitted. Librarians photocopied materials onto "loose paper" for the residents to read in their rooms. In yet other facilities, hardbound books were often not permitted outside the library, if they were permitted at all. Some librarians were able to replace the hard backs with soft covers. Yet another facility did not permit books to be taken out of the library, period. These kinds of higher level rules will certainly influence the kind of library policies that can be developed.

A wide range of security restrictions in juvenile corrections facilities affects how much access youth actually have to books and reading. Some detention centers accept books only from publishers to avoid the possibility of hidden contraband entering the facility. Others accept donations from the public as well as weeded materials from other libraries with little oversight.

LIBRARY SERVICE AGREEMENTS

Formal contracts or agreements between the library service organization and the facility can help clarify the role of the library in the facility, as well as establish legitimate procedures. Not all of the libraries in this study had formal service agreements, either verbal or written.

The library's general charge may be as simple as a verbal agreement between the facility director and the volunteer group that brings donated books from time to time. Some libraries have more formal written contracts between the corrections division and the local public library or school district stipulating various responsibilities and functions.

The purpose of a service agreement is usually to specify the purpose and mission of the library organization within the facility, as well as specific responsibilities, and the reporting relationships within the organization. Service agreements can cover hours of service, location of materials and service, staff or volunteer access to various parts of the facility, collection development guidelines, and/or rules for activities such as Internet access and printing. Some facilities may use the service agreement context to provide the library with policy guidance, sometimes as simple as a list of banned books or types of forbidden content such as depictions of sex, violence, drug use, weapons, or gang/street life. Others have more detailed information, such as procedures for handling challenges to materials.

Meeting with staff and administrators to discuss service agreements can provide an opportunity to talk about expectations and plans as well as points of contact. This is also a good opportunity to review previous problems and discuss solutions.

Three model juvenile detention library service agreements are reproduced with permission in Appendix A, representing policies used by two public library branches and a school library.

COMPUTING IN DETENTION

Learning to use computers and learning to find information using computers are just as important for detained youth as they are for teens and young adults outside. One detention resident stated that the library can "not only show us what is waiting for us in the technological world, but it will also give us a chance to use devices to which we're not accustomed" (Davis 2000: 60). Internet access may or may not be available in a detention library, however; most of the libraries studied for this project did not have computers with Internet access for the youth to use freely. One librarian summed up her frustration with the lack of access: "How can we teach 21st-century information skills without access to the Internet?"

That said, computers with Internet access are increasingly available in detention classrooms, and some facilities make use of online instruction and information resources to supplement in-class teaching. Still, basic access to computers, let alone to the Internet, remains a major challenge for many librarians in detention settings.

The reasons for this are complex. Physical equipment is one issue: Internet access within a typical facility might be provided by the juvenile justice division or probation side of the organization, and they can be reluctant to provide residents with access to components that can be made into weapons. Computer use itself is another issue: while computer activity within a classroom seems to be viewed as less problematic, corrections staff may feel that online activities elsewhere (such as in a library) cannot be adequately monitored. In addition to sending or receiving unauthorized e-mail or instant messages, staff may feel that youth with programming skills might try to hack into a networked system. Residents were not permitted to use computers to communicate with the outside world in any of the facilities in this project.

It can be a challenge in this kind of environment to educate corrections staff on the value of resources accessed online that can be used to educate and entertain without posing security risks. Several libraries in this study demonstrated ways of providing access to computers in libraries that addressed the security concerns of facility administrators. Databases can be housed on stand-alone units or isolated networks. Web site content can be cached for residents to access offline. Physical layouts can be designed so staff can observe online activity: in one detention library that did provide computers with Internet access, computer monitors were placed against a wall, always visible to librarians and corrections staff who observe the residents' online activities. Stored history logs were checked to ensure appropriate use.

ORGANIZING MATERIALS FOR ACCESS

How collections are organized and the type of circulation system will likely depend on a number of factors, starting with funding. If you cannot afford funding for software or equipment or for staff to process materials, then the latest automated system with barcode readers and all the bells and whistles is likely out of reach. If the library is a deposit collection or branch of the local public library, or one of the school district's libraries, processing and technology may be supplied through that relationship, complete with interlibrary loan, holds, and delivery services.

Volunteer or outreach services might or might not have a relationship with the public library or school district, and could be free to design their own methods for keeping track of materials, typically on a shoestring. For volunteers who collect donated books from the community, just transporting the materials to the facility and getting them onto living unit bookshelves will be a huge achievement on its own.

Some detention librarians have developed creative ways to get books into residents' hands quickly and cost-effectively. Arrangements such as the genre-label system ease access and simplify library procedures, particularly processing and circulation, and enhance the user's experience while cutting down on costs. Many public and school libraries already identify and organize popular series, genres, and other materials with labeling and special locations to help users find them quickly; this system merely extends that philosophy to the rest of the fiction collection. Formal Dewey decimal numbers could still be used in the nonfiction section, so residents can learn how those collections in libraries on the outside are organized.

EASY ACCESS

The Alameda County Library at the Juvenile Justice Center uses a simple genre-label classi-fication system for its main library and 12 unit libraries. Books are processed quickly with a minimum of staff time: books get a colored dot and an ownership stamp, and they are ready to go. In addition to regular visits to the main library, residents are able to browse deposit collections in their units that are available to them all the time. Residents keep the living unit collections organized on their own.

The genre-label system works well for smaller collections that are located within living units and are not maintained by library staff, and it also works for larger library-based collections. The point is that teens can find the kinds of books they like on their own quickly. It is also a good system for a fast-moving, short-term detention population: recall that youth can move into and out of short-term detention in days or weeks. If residents ask for a particular title, the time to actually get that book into their hands may be fairly lengthy if libraries are relying on "normal" processing procedures: ordering, receiving, cataloging, barcoding, labeling, and covering. In some public library systems, this can take weeks or months. The genre-label system allows a librar-ian to get a title into a youth's hands in as little as a day.

Drawbacks to these kinds of arrangements, like those of any system, reflect the different priorities in easy access arrangements. Users are not necessarily getting quite the same experience as they would if they had to locate author names and titles alpha-betically in a regular public or school library. For youth who are often several grade levels behind in reading, there is an argument for fostering basic literacy by providing the opportunity for residents to learn their way around a Dewey-organized collection. Having a more formally organized collection would also help familiarize residents with typical public library organization, which would be useful when they are released.

A library without a computerized circulation system will also have less accurate circulation and inventory data, and if due dates are flexible or even eliminated the youth will not "learn" to be responsible for returning books on time. Some facility administra-tors and educators who value these more traditional aspects of library service may not be comfortable with looser arrangements. On the other hand, if the priority is to get books into the hands of youth who need to be reading, eliminating due dates is an effec-tive and efficient solution. The libraries in this study ran the gamut from full-up public library cataloging, circulation, and policies to informal, uncontrolled living unit collections refreshed as often as volunteers could visit.

It is a trade-off. The librarians in this study agreed that a chief objective was to "get these kids reading." Rather than focusing on the librarian's need for controlling the collection, easy access arrangements place a higher priority on meeting youths' other needs, such as helping youth feel ownership of books and reading, and a sense of immediacy in getting something to read quickly. Youth can take responsibility for keeping the books in order in their unit, and the books are there all the time. The savings in processing time and supplies can be substantial for the solo practitioner on a shoestring.

Some teachers or administrators might insist (while admitting they know nothing about libraries) that detention libraries should have a computerized checkout system, Dewey classification, and all the trimmings of a "real" library in order for youth to get the experience of using a real library. It is certainly valuable for residents to have that kind of experience, but these priorities need to be balanced with arrangements that will be sustainable as well as workable in your facility:

You need to have a library that is friendly to them—one that satisfies their needs, not yours. Librarians have this need to keep track of every book. You don't need to keep track of every book! These kids just need to have a positive experience with books.

6

Model Programs and Services

We used to show a film every Friday night and called it a program; the administration started frowning on that. A program has to have some kind of cognitive basis. What are they learning from this?

—A detention librarian

Many of the great programs developed for youth in school and public libraries on the outside will be successful in detention. This chapter does not attempt to cover all the potentially engaging and useful programs you might find in a detention library, but presents general descriptions of types of programs that have been successful in the past. Several actual programs are described in detail at the end of the chapter. For basic youth services programming ideas that will likely work in detention, there are many excellent sources of information to draw from (see sidebar).

PROGRAMMING RESOURCES FOR JUVENILE DETENTION LIBRARIES

Alessio, Amy, ed. 2008. *Excellence in Library Service to Young Adults*, 5th ed. Chicago: American Library Association.

Angier, Naomi. 2003. Juvenile Justice Outreach Library Program. *OLA Quarterly* 9 (3): 15.

Angier, Naomi, Rebecca Cohen, and Jill Morrison. 2001. Juvenile justice outreach: Library services at detention centers. *PNLA Quarterly* 66 (1): 16.

Angier, Naomi, and Katie O'Dell. 2000. The book group behind bars. *Voice of Youth Advocates* 23 (5): 331–3.

Bodart, Joni Richards. 2008. It's all about the kids: Presenting options and opening doors. *Young Adult Library Services* 7 (1): 35–45.

Carlson, Linda. 1997. A day in detention. *ALKI* 13 (3): 18.

Davis, Veronica A. 2000. Breaking out of the box: Reinventing a juvenile-center library. *American Libraries* 31 (10): 58–61.

Ganter, J. 2000. Capture the power of reading. *Illinois Libraries* 82 (3): 176–80.

Ishizuka, Kathy. 2003. NY library gives teens a second chance. *School Library Journal* 49 (11): 24.

Jones, Patrick. 2004. Reaching out to young adults in jail. *Young Adult Library Services* 3 (1): 16–19.

Jones, Patrick, Michele Gorman, and Tricia Suellentrop. 2004. *Connecting Young Adults and Libraries: A How-to-Do-It Manual.* New York: Neal-Shuman Publishers.

Life-Changer. 2006. *Library Journal* 131 (5): 18–19.

Madenski, Melissa. 2001. Books behind bars. *School Library Journal* 47 (7): 40–2.

McLellan, Kathy, and Tricia Suellentrop. 2007. Serving teens doing time. *Voice of Youth Advocates* 30 (5): 403–7.

Source: Carlson (1997); Angier and O'Dell (2000); Davis (2000); Angier, Cohen, and Morrison (2001); Angier (2003); Ishizuka (2003); Jones (2004); Life-Changer (2006); Ganter (2000); Madenski (2001); Jones, Gorman, and Suellentrop (2004); Alessio (2008); and Bodart (2008).

Teens in detention have other information and learning needs that are different from those of teens outside. These youth are more likely to have experienced violence, abuse, or neglect, and they are far more likely to have mental health and/or behavior disorders. Learning disabilities are common, and reading skills are mostly below grade level. Basic knowledge of the world, science, history, and current events is often very limited. Since many will not have good family support when they get out, they need information on basic life skills. Teen parents need guidance on parenting.

Although these areas address a diverse set of needs, there are countless ways to incorporate them into library programming. Programs that help youth develop consequential thinking and problem-solving skills, that help them learn about self-control and how to manage anger, and that teach them about interesting things that are going on in the world will be helpful. All of these topics can be approached through many different kinds of activities; here is a sampling:

- Book talks and discussion
- Presentations by authors and other speakers
- Read aloud
- Fun, recreational activities such as music, movies, art, creative writing, and dance

BOOK TALKS AND BOOK DISCUSSION

You have to realize there are these other possibilities: you can present book talks as more than just reading books. What behavior can you help change?

—A detention librarian

Book talks and book discussion are helpful and very popular with teens in detention, whether they make use of recreational, fun topics or contemporary young adult fiction with more serious themes. Book talks and discussion can be developed around any areas relevant to the youth in the facility, but they will be especially successful around stories about people with problems, solutions, and consequences that are familiar.

Discussion guided by cognitive-behavioral treatment principles has been particularly useful in helping participants recognize negative values and beliefs, and develop positive alternatives to antisocial or destructive behaviors.

Youth can be introduced to stories that provide role modeling and examples of life skills they can emulate. Character-based literacy (CBL) programs have youth read stories and examine the characters' choices and thought processes, and use that information to evaluate the choices they have made in their own lives (Dittman 2007). Characters in stories provide a way for teens to objectively explore why people do what they do, and how actions can have consequences. Reading fiction can provide an outlet for youth to identify similarities and differences with characters and environments, and also gain insight into their own situations.

SPEAKERS AND PERFORMERS

Successful speaker programs will engage youth in interesting topics, such as authors whose books teens have enjoyed, and local business owners and regular people in interesting careers. Teens in detention will be particularly interested to hear from individuals who have experienced difficulties and have overcome challenges. Librarians can discover more specific interests by talking to the residents, staff, and teachers; by taking surveys; and by keeping up with what everyone is reading.

CREATIVE WRITING PROGRAMS

Creative writing and poetry are particularly resonant with youth in detention. Some facilities produce literary magazines or other publications to showcase student work. The Hennepin County Library at the County Home School compiles student writing into *Diverse-City*, a literary magazine published regularly. A poetry program, "Poetry in the Round," presents a theme, such as home or family, and each participant writes a line of the poem without seeing what the other lines are:

It's amazing how these poems turn out, I've never seen one that was not fabulous. . . . They read it and see that others have the same feelings they do. It's really great when they see they have worked on something together, they get to see how easy it is to create something, to put your heart and soul into it and produce something that is wonderful.

—A detention librarian

Writing programs such as Writing for Our Lives make use of short stories, journal writing, discussion, and a problem-solving model to help youth learn to self-monitor their behavior and thought processes. The variations on these types of programs are almost endless and provide ample opportunities for collaboration with educators. Character-based literacy programs often include writing along with reading and discussion. Writing for Our Lives is described in more detail at the end of this chapter.

ARTS PROGRAMS

One of the most powerful ways to reach youth in detention is to give them other chances to be creative in addition to writing. Young people in detention have been shown to benefit tremendously from participating in arts programs, improving self-esteem and confidence, responsiveness to others, empathy, communication skills, and problem solving (Ross, Fabiano, and Ross 1988; Office of Juvenile Justice and Delinquency Prevention 1997; Harlin 2011). Arts programs have been especially successful in bolstering positive development for youth who have excessive feelings of alienation, depression, isolation, and powerlessness by helping them learn to express themselves and learn positive coping strategies.

Participation in creative expression through drawing, painting, sculpture, photography, textiles, ceramics, music, movement, and other artistic activities has been shown to reduce emotional risk factors and make future problematic behavior less likely. Contact with actual artists provides teens with positive role models and inspiration.

REENTRY PROGRAMS

While it is primarily the job of exit counselors, probation staff, and/or social workers in the system to provide specific guidance and support to youth who are reentering society, it has been noted often that the juvenile justice system is frequently only able to provide minimal and often uncoordinated services to released youth (Sickmund 2004). Many teens will be 18 years old when they are released, and many will not have adequate family or financial support on the outside. Reduced staff are increasingly faced with overwhelming caseloads and shrinking resources, and cannot provide much beyond basic monitoring services, which do not adequately support the needs of juveniles when they are released (Singer 2009).

Without support, these young adults are in real danger of failure on the outside. Librarians can help in this area by engaging more closely with youth through enhanced readers' advisory and incorporating cognitive-behavioral techniques in programming to foster positive emotional and behavioral development. These types of activities are essential for supporting youth reentry. Gilman specifically calls for increased partnership with other detention staff to achieve these ends (Gilman 2008). Librarians can work with other service providers to help prepare youth for reentry with programming on life skills, community referral services, and many other topics.

Many detention librarians include a wide variety of programming to help youth prepare for when they get out. Just about anything can be tied to reentry for youth: how to balance a checkbook, what to do in your spare time, and hobbies that are productive and enjoyable (and not criminal). Library programs can help youth develop interests that will help them overcome the difficulties they will face in their lives outside:

Books are a great start but it's not enough. They need to be inspired, they need programs on gang intervention, they need books on rights and responsibilities . . . history and literature in my opinion is not enough.

—A detention librarian

Librarians can help prepare youth for reentry by talking about how to use the library when they get out, and by helping them understand what they can use the public and other libraries for. This is one reason some librarians support organizing the detention library to resemble the public library as closely as possible, including using Dewey numbers and having access to computer catalogs and databases to practice learning how to find information. Some facilities will provide local youth with library cards when they are released; in locations where this is not possible, the librarian can at least help the youth find his or her local library and show the youth how to get a library card.

The librarian can partner with probation officers and counselors to enhance the youths' understanding of where and how to find the information they will need once they are out. The librarian can help inform youth of the breadth of community resource and referral services often provided at their local public libraries. Programming that brings in career counselors, employers, and people in interesting jobs to talk about what they do will be instructive and interesting.

Reentry programming topics can include the following:

- How to write a resume and apply for a job
- How to find a place to live
- How to find social services locations (substance abuse treatment, food aid, shelters, probation, crisis hotlines, and counseling centers)
- How to apply to community college
- How to balance a checkbook

READING TO CHILDREN AND PARENTING

Many incarcerated teens are parents, and a range of programs address parenting skills, including reading to children. Librarians can help teens learn about the importance of reading to their children and give them opportunities to practice reading to their children. Some programs provide copies of books and recordings of the parent reading. The recording and the book can be sent home to the child while the parent is in detention.[1]

PRACTICAL MATTERS

It can be challenging to develop writing or other programs that last more than one session when youth are constantly cycling in and out of the system; in short-term detention, librarians may not have the same group of teens more than a week or two in a row. Programs that have youth work on projects more intensively, such as every evening for a week, can be successful if there is administrative support—in particular, making sure facility staff are available to escort youth to and from the program. Flexibility is needed to accommodate interruptions when residents are called for court appearances, family visits, and other appointments.

From the corrections point of view, any and all activities have security issues. Be sure you know your facility's procedures when it comes to inviting in outside speakers or performers. Visitors may need approval from facility administrators, a background check, and/or a security clearance. The guard at the front desk needs to know about the visitor and be prepared to allow that person to enter. Check with the front desk ahead of time as well as on the day of the visit to be sure your visitor is expected.

Corrections staff, guards, counselors, or whoever escorts residents from place to place need to be willing and able to bring the residents to the program at the appointed time. Check with those individuals too to be sure your event is on the schedule. Unforeseen incidents and lockdowns may delay or prevent programs from happening. Be prepared for these unexpected events with a backup plan, and let your visitor know about the possibility of a last-minute cancellation. Most will be very understanding!

Whether you intend to bring in outside speakers or you want to conduct a program yourself, all programs should be discussed with corrections staff and supervisors, particularly if the activity will bring youth from different living units together, or if the program will disrupt the daily routine in any way. Approaches vary on whether gang members are housed together or apart, or whether they can come together for programs. In short, library staff should expect these types of challenges and be able to work with staff to help make library programs happen.

Programming should always be coordinated with the rest of the facility in mind. Some facilities have active schedules with many events going on every day, particularly if there are community volunteer groups involved in providing counseling and various other services. There could be many other programs going on in different areas with different groups. Residents will have court appointments, medical visits, outside visitors, and other interruptions. Opportunities for collaboration with other volunteer groups or service agencies in the facility should be investigated to make the most of available program time, and to develop relevant programs.

INFORMATION LITERACY INSTRUCTION: KEEP IT SIMPLE

Some detention librarians had the opportunity to provide information instruction, often in conjunction with school projects. These instructional activities tended to emphasize the basics; the idea of the Dewey system is new to most of these youth. And while teens in general often seem to be more and more technologically savvy every day, many of these youth did not know how to search the Internet beyond a simple Google search, efforts often frustrated because of poor spelling.

One librarian in this study urged using as much popular culture as possible to make things interesting, using simple examples, and allowing extra time to complete simple worksheets. The instructional role of the librarian for these youth needs to focus on helping to expand their world knowledge as well as nurturing information literacy.

In one session, the librarian used popular basketball players to explore how to look up biographical information, do simple math (if he was 21 in 1995, when was he born?), and critically explore an Internet source. Another librarian was dismayed to learn that few of her students had heard of Louie Armstrong. By the end of the session, however, several teens were developing an interest in jazz and other types of music.

THE ART OF PROGRAMMING

Maggie (not her real name), an outreach librarian to a detention facility without a library, told me the following story. Her usual program in the facility she visited once or twice a month was a 45-minute read-aloud and discussion session, with readings and questions on topics the librarian felt would be interesting to the teens and would stimulate discussion, often including difficult subjects such as coping with bullies, struggling in school, drug addiction, domestic violence, and so on. The program was given during a school class period once or twice a month, with teachers and corrections staff often attending with the teens. Maggie also brought donated books to give to the teens.

Maggie was pretty much on her own to choose readings and discussion questions, which she felt good about doing. On this particular day, she was setting up the room for the program and talking casually with a teacher. She happened to mention the reading and theme for that day's program: teen suicide. The teacher stopped her and spoke up: a resident's sibling had just committed suicide that week—suicide would definitely not be a good choice for that day. Maggie had to work fast to put together an alternative reading and talk session on the spot. Lesson learned: always have a backup plan.

After that experience, Maggie began drawing up schedules of topics and readings well in advance, and made sure the teachers and staff got a copy. She also tried to communicate more frequently with staff about what was going on in the students' lives. This event actually helped facilitate more discussion with other librarians and staff about the ways they could help residents cope with adversities in their lives.

MODEL PROGRAMS

The following section presents examples of model programs and services that have been successful for youth in detention.

Changing Lives Through Literature

Changing Lives Through Literature was created for young adults in an alternative sentencing program by Johnson County Library Outreach, in Johnson County, Kansas. Based on a model program developed in Massachusetts and designed in cooperation with the Johnson County Juvenile Detention Center, the Department of Corrections, and Court Services, the goal in this program was to reduce the number of repeat offenses and parole violations among the youth participating.

This particular program does not occur in a detention center, although it could easily be adapted for that environment. Youth meet weekly in the library with a probation officer, a judge, and a librarian to discuss assigned readings of contemporary young adult fiction. Literature is selected to present situations, problems, and consequences that resonate with the youth. Discussion questions help teens to identify and recognize socially acceptable beliefs and behaviors, and enable them to change their own attitudes.

Prior to 1998 there were no organized activities here. But because of increased interest in juvenile justice reform, the staff in our detention center and a judge became interested in what could be done for the kids in detention. The judge convened a panel of community members to look into it. Our youth services coordinator at the time [in the public library] had seen an article about a program called *Changing Lives Through Literature* for adults, and contacted the judge about it. . . . We modified the program as an outreach service and it's been fabulous now for years.

—A detention librarian

For more information:

Changing Lives through Literature: An Alternative Sentencing Program. http://cltl.umassd.edu/Home-html.cfm

McLellan, Kathy, and Tricia Suellentrop. 2007. Serving teens doing time. *Voice of Youth Advocates* 30 (5): 403–7.

Source: McLellan and Suellentrop (2007).

Read to Succeed

Read to Succeed is a Johnson County Library Outreach program designed for young adults in the Johnson County Juvenile Detention Center, Kansas. In addition to providing paperback books for the residents, library outreach staff visit the center twice a month during the school year (once a week in the summer) to encourage and stimulate reading. Each Read to Succeed session includes book reviews, book talks, and a read-aloud selection. Youth are encouraged to participate in discussions about what they have read, and to make reading a continuing part of their lives.

Sessions last about 45 minutes, and are planned with a theme in mind to deal with issues of concern to teens: peer pressure, betrayal, anger, and prejudice. A short story or a chapter from a book is read to the group of 10 to 15 teens, followed by questions and discussion. Residents and staff are also encouraged to talk about what they have been reading. After the discussion, residents can choose a book to keep from the collection brought by the library staff.

For more information:

McLellan, Kathy, and Tricia Suellentrop. 2007. Serving teens doing time. *Voice of Youth Advocates* 30 (5): 403–7.

Write to Read

Write to Read is a program in the Alameda County Juvenile Justice Center, Alameda County, California. It is a comprehensive collaborative program that brings library services, programs, and literacy to incarcerated youth. The program offers a range of services: small-group discussions about contemporary topics; tutoring for creative projects such as writing song lyrics to set to music; access to books, book talks, and book discussion; information on community resources; visits from authors and speakers who inspire students with books they might not usually read and share meaningful life experiences; and presentations from community organizations dedicated to reducing recidivism.

Write to Read is an award-winning program: it is the winner of the 2006 Coming Up Taller Award, bestowed by the President's Committee on the Arts and Humanities, recognizing an outstanding model of serving the literacy needs of incarcerated youth; the 2006 Library Journal Movers and Shakers Award; the 2005 Alameda County Office of Education Public Service Award; and the 2000 Community Partnership Award from the University of California, Berkeley.

For more information:

Write to Read: Alameda County Youth Literacy at the Juvenile Justice Center. http://juviewrite2read.aclibrary.org.

Writing for Our Lives

Writing for Our Lives was piloted in Massachusetts in 1994 in the Northeastern Correctional Center, an adult minimum security prison, with the goal of reducing recidivism by teaching pro-social self-concepts, problem solving, impulse control, decision making, and social perspective taking. The program has been adapted successfully in several juvenile detention facilities, including Alameda County Juvenile Justice Center.

Youth in the program meet regularly to read short stories and discuss the characters' actions and perspectives, characters whose situations reflect circumstances and choices they can relate to, in character-based literacy (CBL) exercises. Youths examine the choices, thoughts, and actions of characters in stories, and apply these to their own lives to help them evaluate their own choices.

In some programs, participants are also guided in self-monitoring their behavior, using daily journal writing to document their awareness and development of pro-social behaviors and attitudes. Participants in the program also complete weekly writing assignments on topics that require that they address their present situations and reflect on how they can succeed as productive members of society. Instructors provide positive written feedback on these assignments. Students also learn a step-by-step method of problem solving called the THINK FIRST method, in which they are presented with a problem scenario and work through a checklist to build their decision-making skills (see box below).

For more information:

Dittman, Katherine. 2007. Between the lines: Girls in detention escape into books. *The Monthly* 37 (7). www.themonthly.com/feature-04-07.html.

THE THINK FIRST MODEL OF PROBLEM SOLVING

Got a problem?

Take stock of the situation:

- How do you feel?
- How do you know how you feel (what are the physical signs or symptoms)?

Identify the problem:

- Do you need more information?
- What do you need to know? How will you find out? Who will you ask or won't ask? Why?

Name facts and opinions.

Know where you stand.

Figure out your goals.

- You may have several; list them all.

Identify possible solutions.

- Will they help you reach your goals?

Reflect upon consequences.

- What might happen?

Think first. Then, act.

Source: Adapted from Blinn, Cynthia. 1995. Teaching cognitive skills to effect behavioral change through a writing program. *Journal of Correctional Education* 46 (4): 148.

Second Chance Books

Second Chance Books is an award-winning collaborative outreach effort of the Austin (Texas) Public Library and the Gardner Betts Juvenile Justice Center. Started in 2003, Second Chance provides two satellite branches of the Austin Public Library with a combined collection of over 4,000 volumes for casual reading. These branches are housed at the short-term and long-term lockup facility of the Juvenile Justice Center.

In addition to the two libraries on site, Second Chance offers book clubs, author visits, art programs, and special presentations for the young adults in these facilities, along

with monthly librarian visits to each unit at the facility to provide reader's advisory services. Regular visits help librarians get to know the residents and build trust. Librarians also provide information about the Austin Public Library to residents who are about to be released to help them get started.

For more information:

Austin Public Library. N.d. Second Chance Books. http://www.ci.austin.tx.us/library/2ndchance.htm.

Free Minds

Free Minds is a book club and writing workshop that introduces incarcerated teens to books, reading, and creative writing in order to support their education and success on reentry. The program is currently offered at the District of Columbia Jail to new juveniles who are charged and incarcerated as adults. Weekly book clubs are offered, and a continuing support program provides books and correspondence with inmates when they transfer to adult prison. A reentry support program connects youth who are released to community resources that will help them achieve their goals. By reaching these youth before they become further involved with violence and crime, the program helps to reduce recidivism by motivating the young men to pursue positive new directions in their education and careers.

For more information:

Free Minds Book Club. http://www.freemindsbookclub.org.

Digital Storytelling

In digital storytelling programs, youth learn about using software to create stories and share them with youth in similar programs around the country, using the Internet. Youth watch videos about young people around the world, and create their own comics, animated movies, and videos. Youth can also be encouraged to tell their own personal stories.

For more information:

http://www.columbian.com/news/2010/dec/27/hoping-for-happy-endings-teenage-offenders-turn-th/.

Reading Fathers

Reading Fathers is a program produced at the Mecklenberg County (North Carolina) Jail North facility for incarcerated teen fathers. Young men meet with a librarian weekly for eight weeks to learn how to read to and share books with their children. Inmates who complete the program are permitted a contact visit with their children at the end of the session.

For related information on dads reading to their children:

http://www.picturebookdad.com/Home_Page.php.

http://www.storybookdads.org.uk.

Born to Read and Read to Me

Born to Read and Read to Me are programs for teen parents in the County Home School in Hennepin County, Minnesota. The programs are designed to teach young parents how to read to their children, and about the value and importance of reading to their children. Participants practice reading, and record themselves reading books aloud. Books and recordings are mailed to the children. Program evaluations have documented dramatic positive changes in teens' attitudes toward bringing their children to the library for story time.

For more information:
http://www.ala.org/ala/mgrps/divs/alsc/issuesadv/borntoread/ALA_print_layout_1 _620021_620021.cfm.

Great Transitions Program: Struggle, Achieve, Change

The Great Transitions Program serves young adult residents of the County Home School (Hennepin County, Minnesota) and is designed to acquaint them with the public library and how its resources can help them make the transition from corrections back into the community. In partnership with the Hennepin County Public Library and other local government agencies, the goal of Great Transitions is to engage youth involved in the juvenile system with the library and help them become avid readers and competent information seekers. Components of the program include Read to Me (geared toward teen parents), information literacy instruction, workshops, author visits, and student creative writing and production of the literary magazine *Diverse-City*. The program also features monthly book talks and mock-Printz awards competitions. Probation meetings for released students are held at the local public library to encourage library use.

For more information:
Great Transitions. http://www.hclib.org/extranet/ala2000/.
Diverse-City. Various years. http://www.hclib.org/teens/Diverse_City.cfm.

A.R.T.C. (Achieving Recovery Through Creativity)

Pronounced "artsy," the A.R.T.C program provides teens in a substance abuse program with opportunities to use visual arts, music, and creative writing to help and encourage them to express complicated or difficult emotions and experiences, and help them develop positive coping strategies for difficult situations. Students work in small groups initially to address a specific issue such as the effect of substance abuse on family, coping with a past trauma, and so on. Students meet to discuss the topic, and then develop creative art projects that allow them to express their thoughts and feelings about the topic in an artistic medium. Journal writing and individual counseling are also provided as part of the program. Students meet again at the close of the program to discuss their projects and personal growth. Opportunities are provided for the students to display their work and talent to the community as well.

For more information:
Achieving Recovery through Creativity. http://www.pfh.org/artc/.

NOTE

1. Librarians implementing programs involving contact with family members (including *Reading Fathers*, *Born to Read*, and *Read to Me*) should work with probation and/or child welfare staff to assure that contact is in keeping with the youth's treatment program and does not violate court orders.

7

Strange but True: Inside the World of Detention Library Collection Development

> The main mission of the Department of Corrections is to protect the public. If I am sitting in my library cataloging and there's a staff support call, I am out the door and I am across the field and I am helping. The next goal is preparing the offenders for reentry. After that we have the correctional library statement: we're here to meet the social, cultural, recreational, and educational information needs of our patrons. There is a reentry component there too.
>
> —A detention librarian

The American Library Association's Standards for Library Services in Juvenile Correctional Facilities states it in plain language: the library inside the correctional facility should not be merely a collection of materials for the use of the juveniles and staff in the facility. It should *sustain, foster, and strengthen the total program of treatment and education* (Association of Specialized and Cooperative Library Agencies and American Library Association 1999). As with other special libraries, library collections and services for detained juveniles should serve both the mission and function of the parent organization as well as fulfill the information needs of the users, in this case, the mission of the institutions educating and treating incarcerated youth, and the information needs of the youth and staff.

Collections therefore have to accomplish a number of things. They should support helping youth develop and improve their consequential thinking and decision-making skills. Materials are needed that will present situations they can reflect on and learn from. Information should be provided that will help youth prepare for success on the outside with better life skills and increased literacy. The collection should have books that are interesting, so youth will be encouraged to read. Finally, the library needs to provide freedom of choice for youth to practice exercising their decision-making skills.

Achieving these goals remains a daunting enterprise for most detention libraries. Evidence in this study suggests that even when agreed-upon selection criteria and procedures for handling challenges exist, they are often difficult to implement. Librarians have reported wholesale bans on entire formats and genres based on problematic content of individual items, as well as staff removing materials on their own without consulting anyone, let alone the librarian. This chapter explores some of the reasons why these circumstances exist in the first place, and suggests some approaches librarians can take to address them.

CENSORSHIP: WHAT'S PROHIBITED AND WHY

Censorship is a fact of life in juvenile detention libraries just as it is in adult corrections: no facility is going to permit items that threaten security or discipline such as *The Anarchist's Cookbook*, or information on constructing weapons, locksmithing, methods of escape, drug making, or brewing alcoholic beverages. Materials advocating violence, profanity, or content that might incite residents to violence or criminal activity are generally not permitted. Sexually explicit materials inappropriate for middle or high school students are not permitted.

The American Library Association standards for libraries in juvenile corrections state that the library should have a policy that defines the criteria to be considered in materials selection, and should specify what constitutes contraband. A surprising discovery in this study was that not many libraries had a formal collection policy. One facility librarian was given a list of "disapproved titles" for guidance; other collection policies merely stated that the library will "not collect materials that glorify or promote violence or crime." Yet other facilities simply did not have any documented rules or procedures for acquiring materials or handling challenges.

At the other end of the spectrum, some facilities had specific and detailed library collection policies developed either by the local public library agency providing service, by a state educational agency charged with schooling in detention, or by the juvenile service center itself. Three of these model policies are reproduced in Appendix A.

In general, these collection policies tend to cover the same general topics governing materials selection as might be found in youth collections outside, such as appropriateness of the material for the age group, reading level, and support for the instructional program in the school. Materials should be of interest to the juvenile population, present accurate information, and provide diverse opinions on controversial issues. These are all typical selection criteria for youth collections.

Collections in detention libraries come under closer scrutiny than libraries outside, however. Common targets for challenges are depictions of street life, gangs, crime, and drug use like those found in street or urban literature. Some corrections staff feel that these works promote dysfunctional or criminal lifestyles, and so any mention at all of these types of anti-social situations is deemed harmful to youth. Images of scantily clad women depicted in graphic novels are another area of contention, particularly for sex offenders. Music, especially hip-hop and rap, frequently comes under attack for profanity or anti-social themes.

The question is: will a collection that is completely sanitized of all these materials meet the needs of incarcerated teens and young adults? We know that teens have different information needs from adults as well as from smaller children, and teens in detention have additional considerations. Collection development policies developed for adult prison libraries are clearly not adequate for juvenile detention libraries. In the same vein, teens in detention are also not "just like" their high school or middle school counterparts on the outside.

STRIKING A BALANCE

Teens in detention have unique information needs. Many young people in detention have had experiences far beyond their years, and can identify with material that contains mature themes of drug abuse, violence, and crime. These kids have "seen things we can't imagine," as one librarian put it. As a result, they want to read about stories and situations that may not be considered "age-appropriate" in a middle or high school library on the outside, and that depict situations deemed "anti-social" and thus contrary to the mission of the facility. Here is the conundrum: in the interest of promoting interest in reading, these teens and young adults need access to materials that resonate with their lives. They need to have materials that interest them. The librarian has to choose materials that balance staff prohibitions with the needs of youth. To do this, librarians must select materials that present realistic situations, as well as a positive message that can be defended to staff:

We know that getting books that kids want and having them read whatever they want is what is going to increase their reading. However, you have to work within the system. . . . I have kids in here every day asking for books on gangs, books on killing. You have to understand the needs of the kids, but also the needs of the school department, the needs of the probation department, and you have to address all those needs. It's challenging because the books have to have action and relevance. But you can find books that also satisfy probation.

—A detention librarian

UNDERSTANDING THE ENVIRONMENT

Balancing the information needs of youth with the goals of detention is not simple or easy. On one level, the basic objectives of detention service providers vary widely from place to place: one juvenile probation officer noted a stark difference between two juvenile detention facilities:

When I worked in Ohio . . . the focus was not on helping the kids get better . . . the role of [probation] was to protect the public. . . . In Butler County [Pennsylvania], however, the services are very progressive . . . our supervisors are always pushing us to be creative and rehabilitative, rather than punitive. (Singer 2009: 280)

The prevailing climate in many juvenile justice organizations seems to emphasize punishment over rehabilitation, however, which lowers the visibility of the library in terms of institutional priorities. Another problem is the lack of funding for training corrections staff to work with youth; levels of staff training vary widely from place to place (Willison et al. 2010). While most states require juvenile probation officers in state facilities to have a bachelor's degree or the equivalent, many counties and municipalities require only a high school diploma for working with youth in detention. Other institutions require a master's degree in criminology, social work, or one of the counseling professions for certain positions.

This unevenness in corrections staff knowledge and training translates into weak understanding overall of the information needs of youth, as well as the role and importance of the library for helping youth. Lack of training is at least partly responsible for the continuing poor conditions in juvenile detention (Singer 2009). As one librarian aptly noted, "I wish some of these so-called counselors [corrections staff] would spend more time counseling and less time jailing."

To further complicate matters, as a general rule, residential facilities for juveniles act *in loco parentis*, or in the role of the parent.[1] Regardless of local implementation, however, most detention personnel are obligated to act in the role of a parent, which includes determining what reading material youth should have access to. The problem that librarians face is how to educate detention staff to take on this role effectively and consistently given the unevenness in their understanding of library priorities and the information needs of detained youth.

Librarians and correctional staff often seem to be coming from opposite ends of the spectrum in terms of understanding the information needs of youth. Public libraries on the outside strive for free access to information for everyone; correctional institutions seek to control freedom, particularly in terms of behavior and independent choice. The library is, in fact, one of the only places in detention where youth can exercise real choice (Oiye 1982). From the point of view of corrections, the freedom of thinking afforded in the library is especially problematic because it involves intangibles like thought, knowledge, and learning that staff cannot control. The library is therefore seen as a dangerous place.

Librarians see things very differently, as Brenda Vogel summarized: "The censorship dilemma undermines the foundation of a librarian's training and instinct. Security as a rationale for censorship sometimes defies rational thinking" (Vogel 1995: 15). Collection development in the detention environment therefore requires more than just acknowledging the institutional mission and creating consonant policies and procedures.

THE BAD WORDS DEBATE: DEFENDING THE COLLECTION

These situations must be turned into opportunities to educate people about public library philosophy. Although some may not agree with the philosophy of the right to read and open access, a clarification of policy often alleviates concerns. (Oiye 1982: 204)

What should librarians do when materials are challenged, as they certainly will be? As in libraries outside, librarians should have a *selection policy* approved by administration as well as a *procedure for handling challenges*, and they should *be prepared* for challenges. The model policy documents in Appendix A contain example selection policies and processes for reconsideration of challenged materials. Wayne Disher's *Crash Course in Collection Development* is a good basic resource for developing selection policy and procedures for handling complaints (Disher 2007). Detailed selection criteria will help clarify selection rationale for staff. Librarians should return to the basic purposes of the detention library in writing the selection policy, and acknowledge the facility's mission. Collection policies can also refer to principles of intellectual freedom expressed in documents such as the ALA Library Bill of Rights, the ALA Statement on Prisoners' Right to Read, and the First Amendment to the Constitution of the United States to support collection decisions.

While it is hard to anticipate every possible type of complaint staff might have with individual items, the following points address some of the typical challenges that have come up recently in various institutions (compiled from the YALSA-LOCKDOWN e-mail archive):

- The librarian needs to be able to defend why certain books are nevertheless important even though they contain some profanity and sex. Is there a positive message? Is there a situation that teens can learn from?
- Whole genres of fiction (such as street literature) or music (such as hip-hop and rap) should not be restricted because some individual items contain profanity, explicit sex, or offensive lyrics. Individual items should be judged independently.

A common (and age-old) opinion among corrections staff is that teens in detention should be provided only with materials that demonstrate "good" behavior or "right" thinking. Limiting access to these kinds of "appropriate" materials (e.g., no profanity, sex, crime, drugs, etc.), however, hamstrings a very important learning tool for youth: freedom of choice. Freedom of choice in the library provides a unique opportunity for young offenders to exercise their decision-making muscles. Youth need to learn discernment: understanding the difference between hearing an angry profanity-laced song and telling the librarian to f—- off is an important distinction. Youth need to learn critical thinking: what is the message of this song? Does it apply to me? Do I agree with it? Is the language appropriate in this context? If so, why?

Creating a sterile environment will do little to help youth learn to cope with their problems. Do we really want to let them out with no more knowledge than when they came in? . . . As far as the sex offenders go, everyone here has a treatment and recovery plan, they know what their triggers are. I would much rather have the library be the place where they can exercise their good decision making muscles. If they make the wrong decision, we are in a safe, controlled environment where there are counselors standing at the ready to get them back on track. . . . A lot of offenders go back out without having learned anything about making good choices.

—A detention librarian

The moderating interaction of librarians and others with youth is the crucial link between providing thought-provoking materials and helping youth develop those critical thinking skills. Consider the wide range of opinion on whether urban fiction is acceptable in a detention collection: some administrators still prohibit the entire genre because of its gritty depictions of street life and violence, while others are more tolerant. The genre has exploded in popularity, particularly among youth in detention because they are interested in reading about situations that resonate with their experiences. Finding the titles that provide action and relevance but that also present a meaningful, positive message is only one part of the task. Librarians also have to provide guidance, and interact with youth as they read these works: "It's not just enough that you offer books, ideally you have to ask them, what do you think?"

Library staff needs to monitor how youth react to the books that they read. What are they learning? What are they thinking? As one detention librarian described it,

How you deal with this is a tough balance. There are some books I don't check out to everyone. But the controversial books are the ones that are often the most meaningful, helping the kids make these awesome connections. I think it's important to take the extra step of talking to the kids about what they are reading. Ideally you should ask them, 'tell me what you're thinking'.

—A detention librarian

Many of these youth also have serious mental health and other problems that librarians need to be aware of. Books are powerful things; librarians need to recognize that some materials might not be helpful to certain teens with problems that they are working to overcome. Sex offenders are an obvious example. Librarians need to work closely with counselors to make sure that the library materials they suggest are in consonance with an individual's treatment plan. This can be more challenging in short-term detention facilities where youth may not even be receiving treatment for mental health or other problems.

BE PROACTIVE: COMMUNICATE!

One librarian was looking forward to introducing graphic novels to the collection in her facility library. Some of the corrections staff were immediately suspicious, and began flipping through the books looking for objectionable material. The librarian took that opportunity to engage staff in conversations about the books, and was ultimately able to shift staff away from the "witch hunt" mentality to a more collaborative "let's read this book together and talk about it" mode. Some items were removed; most stayed.

Amy Cheney emphasizes that establishing trust with the administration and staff will be critical to the librarian's success in demonstrating that the books selected will help everyone fulfill the mission of the institution and not "harm" the youth. She stresses taking a proactive approach to collection development by bringing to administration's attention books that she feels are not appropriate for the collection and removing them. In this way she demonstrates her commitment to the institution's mission to provide appropriate materials, and establishes trust (Cheney 2009).

Now, on the other hand, a book like *Kendra* that has somewhat graphic yet not gratuitous sex scenes is a vitally important teen book, as are other adult books that chronicle graphic experiences with reflection such as *Always Running* or *Long Way Gone*. . . . These have a strong place here and I will fight for them to be here. . . . Triple Crown type books in an adult public library setting are vital [there]; however they cause too much drama in my institution and are not necessary to get the kids happily reading. (YALSA-LOCKDOWN post, February 4, 2009)

Books that speak to the developmental needs of teens are crucial, and librarians need to be able to defend certain works that have value to youth while distinguishing them from gratuitous works that are not needed in the collection:

I have so many books that the youth enjoy reading, and that satisfy their need for street and urban fiction that I don't feel it's necessary to bring in the more graphic sex and violence scenes that seem to be reactive rather than reflective.

—A detention librarian

Careful, clear, and constant communication between librarians and facility staff is essential. The librarians who seemed to have the most success with providing materials banned elsewhere were the ones who had taken the time to talk to corrections staff about why specific books were good choices, and why others were not. Librarians need to build a coherent collection policy and apply it consistently, based on their knowledge of teen and young adult information needs, as well as the special emotional and developmental needs of the incarcerated teen. Librarians need to be able to support their choices with objective information.

This sounds straightforward, but it is not easy. Some corrections staff members (and even some administrators) are simply not readers, and have never considered how reading can help youth learn, grow, and develop. It can be difficult to reach these individuals. Librarians in detention are challenged to create a culture of reading throughout the detention community, not just among the teens.

DEFENDING STREET LIT

Urban literature is aggressively marketed to the minority youth demographic, particularly young African American men. Some critics contend that street lit offers an extremely negative stereotype of the black experience that is not helpful to minority teens in detention. This is not true of the entire genre, however, and librarians need to work to raise consciousness about the differences between works that are merely belligerent and damaging versus those that compel reflection:

As librarians that work with the population that these books are marketed to, it's our responsibility to provide other options, to do the research to find books that our patrons will enjoy, and to stand up against the aggressive and destructive sell of gangsta anything. We need to bring in books, speakers, information, and programs that help youth to think critically and question what their beliefs are and what they are being sold. I think when we stand up and claim our expertise we will be challenged less by probation. (YALSA-LOCKDOWN post)

Support for collection policies can also be found elsewhere in the juvenile justice system. One librarian worked closely with a juvenile court judge, both giving and taking suggestions for books that would be appropriate and meaningful for youth in the system. The judge's interest in and support of the library as a positive and important element in treating youth provided invaluable credibility to the library in that facility. Educators and the myriad social services providers can also become advocates for the library.

BUILDING COLLECTIONS FOR THESE TEENS: SOME NUTS AND BOLTS

Collections for youth in detention draws from several areas: standard sources for youth and young adult collections, plus more specialized attention to areas that address the specific needs of youth in detention. Standard collection development resources include *Booklist, School Library Journal, Teen Urban Fiction*, and numerous booklists published by ALA and other organizations. *Connecting Young Adults and Libraries* by Jones, Gorman and Suellentrop is an excellent resource covering the panoply of young adult collections and services, and provides a hefty bibliography of collection development source material, as well as young adult services resources in general (Jones, Gorman, and Suellentrop 2004).

Additional selected online collection development resources are included in Appendix B. All these materials offer solid advice for developing well-rounded and appropriate teen and young adult collections.

The collection for this population needs to go beyond basic young adult requirements, however, and we can do this by drawing from the earlier discussion on the information needs of youth in detention (see Chapter 3). The collection needs to contain materials that help teens address:

- Social and emotional development
- Physical, safety, and security needs
- Intellectual and cognitive development
- Health and sexuality
- Creativity

To help youth address their specific cognitive and behavioral problems, the library should provide materials on:

- Consequential thinking, empathy, and understanding consequences of actions and how actions affect others
- Critical reasoning, decision making, and problem solving
- Substance abuse
- Mental and behavioral health, and anger management

Because so many of these teens have not had adequate educational opportunities, the library should offer information on:

- GED preparation
- Community college applications
- Communication college curriculum
- Vocational education
- Employment
- Housing, social services, and other community resources
- Life skills
- Parenting

Music offers a vitally important connection to peer culture for youth who are temporarily isolated from society, sometimes for lengthy periods. Music helps youth maintain feelings of connectedness that can help them adapt when they get out.

Finally, and perhaps most importantly, the detention collection needs to nurture a fundamental interest in reading. Krashen supports free and voluntary reading as one of the "most powerful tools" in language education (Krashen 2004). Many librarians in this study strongly advocated providing youth with whatever reading material they were interested in, without judgment. Krashen's evidence suggests that even one single positive reading experience can "create a reader." In this study, a high school principal remarked that teachers in high schools on the outside can tell when a youth in detention has been reading because they notice the increase in their verbal skills. Librarians have observed this as well; recall the story of Jose, an incarcerated youth who began reading in the juvenile corrections center with a comic book and was gradually working his way through the entire library collection: "I'm using my time in here to educate myself."

NOTE

1. Application of this rule can vary somewhat. One librarian noted that the staff at their facility acts as guardians for the committed youth but not for the pre-adjudicated detained youth.

8

From Conflict to Cooperation: Making It Work in Detention

> My work with this administration and the prior administration has been key to the progress we've made. If you have a great library and great staff but you don't have the administration on board you are dead in the water. . . . You have to realize how critical your diplomacy and advocacy skills are. Librarians might be excited about picking out books, and excited about helping kids in jail, but they might not necessarily be excited about being a supreme diplomat. It is absolutely essential.
>
> —A detention librarian

Successful librarianship in detention goes beyond handing out books and talking with the youth who visit the book truck. Relationships with other staff in the facility are vital to the success of the library on a day-to-day basis, making sure youth can attend programs and have access to the library. The detention library "community" includes more than the youth; it potentially includes everyone who has some contact with the facility: teachers, counselors, probation officers, corrections staff, judges, lawyers, parents, other volunteers, and even the chaplain.

Ideally the library should be accessible to all these individuals to assist them with information within the context of the juvenile detention library mission. Establishing positive relationships with other staff can help the librarian communicate the vital role of the library for the youth, and create support for library activities.

Unfortunately, as we have seen so far, most juvenile detention libraries do not operate in perfect worlds. The detention librarian works in an environment that has peculiar social and institutional characteristics that often seem to operate at cross purposes to library goals of access to information and free reading. Libraries and juvenile corrections institutions are very different organizations, with different purposes, histories, and cultures. Finding common ground can be a challenge.

For one thing, juvenile detention facilities typically involve multiple government agencies managing multiple services: corrections departments are concerned with security; the health department and/or social services agencies might be involved with assessing and treating juveniles for physical health problems, substance abuse, or mental health problems; and education is concerned with teaching in the classrooms (and often the books in the library). Various other volunteer and/or quasi-governmental organizations might be providing still other programs and services.

This often disconnected system is rooted in a fundamental dichotomy: the two major types of agencies responsible for working with troubled youth, child welfare and juvenile justice, have rarely worked well together. Social welfare seeks to protect youth from harm; the justice system seeks to protect the public from harm caused by the youth (Singer 2009).

Not only do these agencies not work well together: it is not unusual for government divisions to have competitive rather than collaborative relationships. Not surprisingly, policies coming out of these different agencies often conflict. On just a practical level, librarians need to make sure that library policies do not get in the way of any other department's administrative rules. This is not an easy task.

Library cooperation with other departments and agencies is vitally important in the detention facility for many reasons beyond just getting support for library activities and creating consonant policies. Research has shown that better cooperation improves outcomes for individuals involved in the criminal justice system, especially juveniles (Foster-Fishman et al. 2001; Rivard and Morrissey 2003; Lehman et al. 2009). Improved library-facility cooperation also benefits overall organizational functioning.

Leaving aside this systemic dysfunction for the moment, why have librarians found cooperation so difficult to achieve? Part of the problem is likely that librarians (as well as other staff) do not have a clear understanding of what cooperation entails, or how to overcome obstacles in cooperation, particularly in complicated multi-agency environments like juvenile detention. Research on cooperation and collaboration involving libraries in detention is limited, let alone on collaboration across multiple agencies of the sort that operate in juvenile corrections or on the types of problems that come up. However, other disciplines have developed useful definitions on cooperation and its barriers, and what organizations in general can do to foster good cooperative relationships.

First, what exactly do we mean by "cooperation"? In the public administration arena, cooperation occurs when two or more entities work together toward a common goal, or work jointly with others for mutual benefit (Bardach 2001; Vogel et al. 2007). "Collaboration" is a more focused and specific relationship that might require contribution of resources from involved parties, merging of effort and decision making, and a joint reason for cooperation (Linden 2002). A key identifying element of true collaborative effort is often a shared goal or vision for which all participants will take ownership and/or credit. The question is: do libraries and the other agencies within juvenile detention share such a goal or vision?

The evidence in this study suggests that they do not. Each institution involved with the juvenile justice system—the police, the courts, probation, detention facilities themselves, and the myriad social service agencies that are involved with children's placement in detention (including libraries)—has its own responsibilities, expectations, and goals. These agencies usually make independent decisions about interventions into children's lives without shared or consistent goals (Rosenheim 2002). What is more, individual agencies do not typically negotiate their own objectives with other offices, nor do they share value systems. Finally, different agencies tend to compete for public attention and resources rather than coordinate their needs.

Historical and political factors are also at work in the juvenile justice system. Policies and public opinion have swung regularly between the protection of vulnerable children and the punishment of "bad" children. The early juvenile courts at the turn of the 20th century one hundred years ago stressed the need for children to be treated sympathetically, but that perspective has long since shifted to the punitive end of the spectrum (Rosenheim et al. 2002). Since the late 1970s, the justice system has increasingly criminalized delinquent children, especially during the 1990s in the push to "get tough" on youth violence and crime (Griffin 2003). A sizeable gap remains between the current punitive goals of juvenile corrections and the educational and rehabilitation goals of libraries in detention.

Cooperation across agencies that differ significantly in organizational goals and culture, such as libraries and juvenile corrections, presents special challenges. Radical differences in values can be difficult to overcome. High-level support for activities outside one's own department may be lacking, and without support it can be difficult to obtain needed buy-in from staff in other departments. Rigid bureaucratic structures can obstruct funding. Some organizational cultures actively resist change and thwart information sharing, making communication very difficult. Collaboration can be hindered by management problems such as poorly designed or understaffed programs, lack of clear guidelines, and inadequate resources. Evidence from this study seems to indicate that these issues exist in detention too.

Cooperation between individuals can be stressful if relationships are too informal or if responsibilities and commitments are not well defined (Gunawardena, Weber, and Agosto 2010). One investigation of collaborations involved with providing mental health services found that while there were many informal relationships across agencies, there were few formal relationships, little centralization, and fragmented and insufficient resource flows (Polivka et al. 2001). In a study of child protection agencies and mental health service providers, barriers to cooperation included mutual mistrust across professional domains, inadequate resources, gaps in processes, and unrealistic expectations (Darlington, Feeney, and Rixon 2005). In another study of a child welfare substance abuse program, researchers observed deeply ingrained mistrust and a lack of understanding of the other agencies values, goals, and perspectives (Green, Rockhill, and Burns 2008). Similarly, parties in different disciplines may have different expectations for participation and use different vocabularies that are not understood by all (Gunawardena, Weber, and Agosto 2010).

The evidence in this study suggests that libraries in detention experience many of these issues. What can libraries do to overcome these difficulties?

PARALLEL CHALLENGES IN SOCIAL WORK

Comparing the roles that social workers play in the juvenile justice system to those of librarians provides some guidance. Professional standards and practice guidelines for social work have strongly supported involving social workers in the rehabilitation, treatment, and care of delinquent youth (Springer and Roberts 2009), just as the current standards for libraries promote a strong and proactive role supporting and strengthening detention facilities' "total program of treatment and education" (Association of Specialized and Cooperative Library Agencies and American Library Association 1999).

However, the clinical needs of youth in the justice system are frequently dispersed across multiple areas such as child welfare, substance abuse, mental health, and education. Further, treatment providers and educators typically do not consult with each other, or with social workers or librarians. Goals established by the courts are usually focused more on punishing the infraction rather than on treating any co-occurring clinical issues (such as mental health or substance abuse), and tend to take priority in case planning. Whether or not a youth has been found guilty of an offense as opposed to being merely detained pre-adjudication also affects whether a youth will have access to treatment at all.

Finally, the multiple needs of juveniles do not necessarily fit into the predetermined categories of services offered by various agencies (Provan et al. 2004). A youth may have emotional difficulties stemming from a dysfunctional family environment, low literacy due to an untreated learning disability, and substance abuse problems. Service integration across areas is particularly important for vulnerable populations such as children and minorities, for whom service coordination and tracking are more challenging, and who have likely been marginalized in the past. At the current time, services for juveniles continue to be poorly integrated.

The care mandates of social work suggest the need for a more engaged role in the juvenile justice process, yet the role of social workers is often restricted to outpatient or crisis counseling outside of the detention environment. Training in the specific skills needed to operate in the juvenile justice system is also not provided by most schools of social work (Neighbors, Green-Faust, and Beyer 2004). In a similar manner, the librarian's role in detention is often relegated to merely providing reading materials without the opportunity to provide additional useful services such as readers' advisory, literacy instruction, book discussion, or referral to resources on the outside after reentry. Very few graduate programs in library science offer programs in corrections librarianship; fewer include adequate coverage of juvenile detention librarianship (posted to the *Open Lib/Info Sci Education Forum* email list JESSE@LISTSERV.UTK.EDU, December 14, 2009).

ADMINISTRATIVE COMPLEXITIES

The librarians in this study described several areas where lack of cooperative relationships seemed to hinder library services most often: complex administrative housing and service delivery arrangements, poor communication, and differences in expectations all served to limit the library's effectiveness.

First, many facilities house different categories of residents, such as youth who are detained awaiting adjudication, as well as youth who have been committed to a period of detention for their offense. Also, youth who are guilty of status offenses are often housed in the same location as delinquent youth.

An important problem for library services has to do with housing these multiple populations. Within some facilities, different agencies can be responsible for youth depending on where they are in the judicial process, that is, pre-adjudication versus committed (see Chapter 2 for a description of the juvenile justice process). Two or more different administrative bodies could be responsible for education, such as a facility school for committed residents run by the local youth services or corrections agency, as well as a branch of the local school district for those students who are detained pre-adjudication, all in the same facility. How the librarian interfaces with these entities varies depending on local custom, resource availability, and/or the personalities of the librarians and the administrators. One institutional library consultant described such a situation this way:

Sometimes there are two different school systems under one roof. The school district is responsible for the detained residents, and once they're committed, the Department of Youth Authority is responsible for their education . . . there are two sets of teachers, two sets of classrooms, usually separate. In some cases they have worked it out, but it's a challenge for them deciding who's responsible for the library. It's also a challenge to provide similar services to these two different populations. In one facility here, the principal in charge of the committed residents doesn't want to take responsibility for the library, and neither does the school district principal. So they just have a [corrections] staff person take responsibility on top of their other duties such as security, administrative assistant, etc., or have teachers check out books in their spare time. . . . The challenge for me in working with different agencies is that I am under the Department of Education but the facilities are under the Department of Youth Corrections [DYC]. In some places, I have to figure out if I am going to work with a school district principal or teacher, or with a DYC principal, and/or a variety of staff too. . . . The fact is I am in a support role and I can't go in and tell people what to do.

—A library consultant

COMMUNICATION ISSUES

Wide disparities in the quality of communication existed between librarians and corrections staff in a number of facilities. A few reported good relationships with staff. In most facilities, however, poor communication affected understanding of facility rules and procedures, as well as juveniles' use of the library and access to materials. Several librarians reported not being informed about how decisions were made regarding who gets to visit the library and when or why library visiting privileges were denied. One librarian commented:

In theory, each class goes down [to the library] once a week. But it gets very confusing, I am never quite sure what's going on. There is always confusion. Even when you ask [corrections staff], they are always vague. The residents are supposed to go down once a week, not with their class but with a guard. Some guards are really good, but it varies. Sometimes they don't show up, and I never know why they don't come. . . . There are many different layers of staff, and I am never quite clear on whose job is what.

—A detention librarian

A contrasting view was provided by another librarian, whose working relationships with facility staff seemed much more positive and inclusive:

I feel very lucky that staff is supportive. When I first got here it was difficult because we are so isolated. [Corrections] staff had not been in an urban library in a long time, and they didn't understand it is not a quiet place, they just wanted to see kids sitting quietly and reading. . . . A lot of it has to do with trust. You need to build rapport and trust with the staff, so they know you are not going to do anything crazy. Staff trusts me now. . . . I think I work well with them, and I collaborate with the school also and that works well. They include me in what they do.

—A detention librarian

DIFFERING EXPECTATIONS

Evidence showed differences in expectations between librarians and other staff regarding basic conventions of library service such as the purpose of a library and how well library services were integrated into educational or other programs. Not surprisingly, there were also sharp differences in expectations concerning what types of materials the residents should be permitted to read. These differences also varied widely across facilities, with higher levels of library integration and understanding in certain facilities and lower levels in others. One librarian characterized the lack of understanding of the library's purpose and goals at her facility this way:

The other obstacle is just getting the juvenile detention staff sort of on board, it's the censorship. It's hard to get them to understand how important these books are. We know we need to get the kids interested in reading. We need to get the staff to understand what teen fiction is all about, why it's important to get kids thinking about these things. I haven't been able to address that at all.... One person who works at the detention center came to my storytime [at the public library] and went off on a tirade about how we were bringing in books that were harming the children.... I took that opportunity to say, "Wow, I understand how you feel" and then I tried to share my perspective on why we do what we do.

—A detention librarian

The librarian has a complex and difficult role to play in terms of balancing library objectives with corrections objectives. The mind-set of the corrections environment remains punitive, while libraries focus on access and free choice. Several librarians talked about the difficulties of establishing trust with detention staff members who want to restrict reading to certain kinds of "beneficial" materials while censoring "dangerous" or "harmful" literature. One librarian shared this perspective:

We love to say, as a profession, we are all about giving access, but in reality that doesn't happen, even in the public library. You've got to play nicely with the governing agency, while upholding library ethics. This is only compounded in prison. Not only do you have the school agencies breathing down your neck, you have law enforcement.... You have to maintain the trust of the non-librarian staff in those agencies. It is much more complicated and incredibly difficult.

—A library consultant

The variety in differences across institutional perspectives could also be a function of the variation in a number of different institutional characteristics, including organizational culture, leadership, and the type of residents. A library consultant noted these differences across facilities:

Going out to these other two facilities, you will see how very different correctional facilities can be from each other ... all pursuing the same mission but in terms of how they do it, there are many different ways ... because the culture is different, the administration is different, the offender population is different.

—A library consultant

At one end of the spectrum are detention center cultures that seem almost antagonistic to libraries:

[The challenge is] working in an environment where books are contraband. Another is working in an environment with adults who don't believe in children's right to read and who don't uphold it. . . . Third, coming into an environment where people do not use libraries or see the need for libraries.

—A detention librarian

On the other hand, a few detention facility environments seem to be far more conducive to fostering library services and programs. In these places, a strong connection seemed to exist between the effectiveness of the library program and the coordination among librarians and facility staff, particularly facility directors and educators, as described by one librarian:

After many discussions with my supervisors (the associate facility superintendent and the director of the education program), we decided to concentrate our curriculum on the reading aspect. . . . Many of the students here have not been to library, ever, in their lives. Reading is a big priority of the school curriculum. We are trying to coordinate with the academic coordinator here to improve student reading as much as we can while they are here. . . . The curriculum for these guys is concentrated on giving them current reading material, interesting reading material, and encouraging them to read.

—A detention librarian

Finally, the time and effort needed to build trust and connections across these deep differences are often difficult to come by given high staff turnover in juvenile corrections. High turnover among probation and corrections administrators and staff poses a constant challenge to developing productive and supportive relationships. Part-time outreach or volunteer librarians who visit the facility only once or twice a month or less will have even more difficulty establishing and maintaining these kinds of relationships because they do not have as much time to spend interacting with staff.

Despite these difficulties, many juvenile corrections administrators realize efforts need to be made to improve cooperation. Librarians who have established good working relationships all around will find it easier to gain staff support when needed. Librarians can build trust by keeping staff informed of library activities that affect them, being informed of their professional issues and problems, and asking their opinion about how to handle situations in their areas of expertise. It is important to understand that although the library is not the top priority in detention, it can support and contribute meaningfully to helping the facility fulfill its institutional mission.

Librarians can nurture cooperation in many ways:

- Be on board with the institutional mission. Show how the library contributes to security, behavior management, rehabilitation, and education.
- Get to know other service providers in the organization.
- Build trust across departments.
- Be part of the team; make time for in-service training with corrections officers and others.
- Strive to raise consciousness on what the library does and can do for the youth as well as for staff.
- Advocate for access to reading for your youth.
- Establish a library review board to help negotiate collections challenges.
- Create a reading culture among adult role models: support and nurture reading among staff.

RELATIONSHIPS WITH TEACHERS

I am completely reliant on the good graces of the school district teachers who are willing to give up their class time to allow library services to happen. The probation department does not make time for the library during the kids' days.

—A detention librarian

Librarians in this project expressed a range of level of communication with teachers. In some places there is active collaboration, with librarians assembling information sessions to go along with lesson plans in the classroom. In other places, planning is done in the hallway, on the fly, with little time for preparation. Teachers may sometimes have some of the same narrow opinions on the appropriateness of library materials mentioned earlier. Many teachers are overworked and often pressed for time. Turnover among teachers can be high.

In any case, librarians and teachers tend to have similar goals for working with residents, and can work together productively to help youth. A teacher may be able to let a librarian know that a youth is having a hard time that day and might benefit from some extra attention. Or the librarian might notice tension brewing and be able to share that with the teachers. In this study, librarians' relationships with teachers tended to be more collegial than those with corrections staff:

Philosophically and psychologically, I share a perspective and moral view more with teachers than I do with the counselors [corrections staff]. . . . I can't imagine this job without them. They are the reason the kids even get to come to the library.

—A detention librarian

CREATING A CULTURE OF READING

Librarians in this study brought it up more than once: the youth are not the problem, it's the staff: corrections staff who take away books, who belittle a youth's reading choice, and who insist that "these kids can't read anyway" or that they don't "deserve" to have books: these are unfortunate and frustrating aspects of some corrections cultures. Librarians have to look on all their interactions with staff as potential opportunities to gently educate about library philosophy and the right to read:

The hardest thing is not the kids. The kids do not give me a hard time, the kids are a joy. The probation department as represented by many of the counselors. . . . I feel like they are sometimes getting in the way of the kids' rehabilitation themselves.

—A detention librarian

Librarians can encourage staff to read by providing them with advice on good books: the graveyard shift certainly has plenty of time for reading. A great goal is to get the staff reading the books that the youth are also interested in, and to encourage interaction between staff who read and the youth. One librarian invites staff to participate in book discussion. The more reading adult role models the kids are exposed to, the better. The youth will respect the corrections officers and teachers who are readers, and who take the time to talk to them about what they are reading:

Your job is to get your community engaged. That's outreach. I had a janitor come up to me and say 'you have so many good books in your library I've started reading.' The more adults that are reading around the kids, the more adults they interact with who will say, hey I read this book you might like, that's what kids need to see.

—A detention librarian

Positive relationships need to be nurtured throughout the facility by getting to know the staff and cultivating relationships with the administrators. In the general scheme of things, libraries are often fairly low on the list of priorities in the facility. Recall the performance standards discussed earlier: no mention of libraries at all. This means librarians have to advocate for the library by educating administrators and staff on the role of the library in the institution, why the library is important, and how the library's mission supports the institutional mission:

If you have the support of the community it is very difficult to get rid of the library. . . . Your job is to engage your community. That's outreach to the community.

—A detention librarian

9

Conclusion: The Future Role of Librarians Serving Teens in Detention

Is there agreement on the role of libraries in juvenile detention? Perhaps not completely. Many detention libraries and library services have evolved to meet very specific, local needs that fit the unique characteristics of individual institutions. Librarians interviewed for this study framed their purpose and function across a range of goals:

- To get teens reading and increase literacy
- To give juveniles something to do to fill time
- To use reading and access to information to help youth learn to make better decisions and avoid wrong behaviors
- To help them develop informational skills they will need when they get out
- To incorporate corrections and rehabilitation functions in the library environment

A lot of progress has been made. Librarians understand much more now about the importance of reading and literacy for youth, especially troubled youth. More is known about the information needs of these youth, such as developing consequential thinking, becoming accountable for their actions, and becoming competent to succeed, and how libraries can meet those needs. Librarians have had success in creating partnerships with many caring organizations to bring meaningful programming to teens in detention that helps them in countless ways. In some facilities, librarians have even helped broaden narrow, negative perceptions to help youth gain better access to meaningful books and literature.

Nevertheless, more work is needed. Too many facilities are without libraries; many more are without trained librarians to develop and guide needed programs. This is only one deficit, however. The evidence in this study suggests a much more powerful and compelling role for libraries and librarians within juvenile justice.

As Isaac Gilman urged, the stage is set for librarians to embrace more fully the principles of balanced and restorative justice, and to provide more than just recreational reading and literacy services (Gilman 2008). We need to recognize and develop our positive, vital role in what is potentially the most important development in juvenile justice history. Balanced and restorative justice is the first approach to truly provide a coherent framework that supports positive youth development while recognizing the need for accountability and community involvement. Library engagement with youth in detention needs to embrace these principles through new partnerships with educators, welfare services, justice professionals, and others who care about youth.

Balanced and restorative justice is a system and approach that will help bring together entities and their services that are currently disassociated and often marginalized, to the detriment of the youth in the system. By uniting under the three basic principles of balanced and restorative justice—accountability, community, and competency—librarians can find support and rationale for connecting with victim advocacy organizations, social welfare providers, educators, and the justice system. Librarians can be part of a unifying force helping to bridge the gap among these disparate groups serving the many juveniles in the system who are in danger of slipping through the cracks between child welfare services and the justice system. The balanced and restorative justice model cannot solve all the problems in the system without the unifying involvement of librarians.

PARTING WORDS

The library is the decompression chamber, preparing patrons for the transition to community, from being an inmate to becoming a citizen. The library represents opportunity. Making advantage from this opportunity requires individual, voluntary commitment.... This is an experience different from any other in prison. This is the librarian's contribution to the prison community and to society. I consider it to be a valuable contribution.

—Brenda Vogel (1938–2010) (Vogel 1995)

Appendix A

Model Policies

Nancy S. Grasmick
State Superintendent of Schools

200 West Baltimore Street • Baltimore, MD 21201 • 410-767-0100 • 410-333-6442 TTY/TDD

**Juvenile Services Education Program Library Media Services
Program Overview:**

The Juvenile Services Education Library Media Services Program will be an integral part of the total instructional program for each student. As such, in partnership and collaboration with the Maryland Department of Juvenile Services (DJS), the goals of the Library Media Services (LMS) program are to provide:

- instructional opportunities that meet the appropriate content standards of the Maryland Library Media State Curriculum, the Maryland Technology Literacy Standards for Students, and the American Association of School Librarians - *Standards for the 21st-Century Learner.*
- every student access to a functional, well-equipped Library Media Center that supports the goals outlined in *The Standards for School Library Media Programs in Maryland.*
- instructional and professional support to the faculty and staff of the JSEP.

Given the realities of the teaching/learning environment of schools, the development of information and technology literate high school graduates must be viewed as a responsibility shared by all members of the learning community; i.e., library media specialists, content area teachers, administrators, parents, and students.

To succeed in our rapid-paced, global society, our learners must develop a high level of skills, attitudes and responsibilities. All learners must be able to access high-quality information from diverse perspectives, make sense of it to draw their own conclusions or create new knowledge, and share their knowledge with others (AASL, 2009).

The students in the Juvenile Services Education Program need to develop these skills as part of their foundation for responsible behavior and success in the community.

MARYLAND STATE DEPARTMENT
OF EDUCATION
Juvenile Services Education Program

MISSION

The program delivers a continuum of learning experiences to accelerate achievement, personal development, and readiness for a successful future.

VISION

The Juvenile Services Education Program will be recognized as a national leader in the education of detained and committed youth.

GUIDING PRINCIPLES

1) Balanced Approach	We commit to a balanced approach in the education program that ensures academic acceleration and program accountability, and provides opportunities for youth to develop into responsible adults.
2) Integration	We establish and deliver a high-quality education program that provides dynamic and individualized academic, career and college readiness services geared to the learning level of the students.
3) Engaging Instruction	We deliver high-quality, engaging instruction provided by certified teachers.
4) Social Development	We provide opportunities for youth to develop processes for positive personal and social development skills within their community.
5) Partnership	We participate fully in a shared leadership system that works cooperatively with the Department of Juvenile Services (DJS) and other stakeholders to provide youth with optimal educational experiences.
6) Accountability	We hold all staff and the program accountable for established school improvement and achievement outcomes.
7) Alignment	We provide instructional strategies to integrate applied academics into all program components that engage students in active and relevant learning based on MSDE state standards.
8) Value Personnel	We value the individual strengths, needs, and backgrounds of our students and staff. We advocate on behalf of ourselves, our staff and our students to acquire needed resources and opportunities for professional growth and development.

Nancy S. Grasmick
State Superintendent of Schools

200 West Baltimore Street • Baltimore, MD 21201 • 410-767-0100 • 410-333-6442 TTY/TDD

JSEP Library Media Services Instructional Policy, December 2009

Prepared by Roberta Reasoner, Library Media Coordinator, Juvenile Services Education Program
Maryland State Department of Education

Maryland State Department of Education (MSDE)
MISSION
The mission of the Maryland State Department of Education is to provide leadership, support, and accountability for effective systems of public education, library services and rehabilitation services.

Juvenile Services Education Program (JSEP)
MISSION
The program delivers a continuum of learning experiences to accelerate achievement, personal development, and readiness for a successful future.

VISION
The Juvenile Services Education Program will be recognized as a national leader in the education of detained and committed youth.

Juvenile Services Education Program Library Media Services Instructional Policy:
The Juvenile Services Education Library Media Services Program will be an integral part of the total instructional program for each student. As such, in partnership and collaboration with the Maryland Department of Juvenile Services (DJS), the goals of the Library Media Services (LMS) program are to provide:

• instructional opportunities that meet the appropriate content standards of the Maryland Library Media State Curriculum, the Maryland Technology Literacy Standards for Students, and the American Association of School Librarians - *Standards for the 21st-Century Learner.*
• every student access to a functional, well-equipped Library Media Center that supports the goals outlined in *The Standards for School Library Media Programs in Maryland.*
• instructional and professional support to the faculty and staff of the JSEP.

Given the realities of the teaching/learning environment of schools, the development of information and technology literate high school graduates must be viewed as a responsibility shared by all members of the learning community; i.e., library media specialists, content area teachers, administrators, parents, and students.

To succeed in our rapid-paced, global society, our learners must develop a high level of skills, attitudes and responsibilities. All learners must be able to access high-quality information from diverse perspectives, make sense of it to draw their own conclusions or create new knowledge, and share their knowledge with others (AASL, 2009).

The students in the Juvenile Services Education Program need to develop these skills as part of their foundation for responsible behavior and success in the community.

Juvenile Services Education Program Library Media Services Instructional Procedures:

The Maryland State Department of Education JSEP Library Media Program materials are selected by the JSEP to implement, enrich, and support the educational program for the student. Materials must serve both the breadth of the curriculum and the needs and interests of individual students. The JSE P is obligated to provide for a wide range of abilities and to respect the diversity of many differing points of view. To this end, principles must be placed above personal opinion and reason above prejudice in the selection of materials of the highest quality and appropriateness.

I. Each School Library Media Center shall be managed by a professional MSDE certified Library Media Specialist or Instructional Assistant. MSDE shall provide school library services at all major juvenile centers through a certified Library Media Specialist. The Library Media Specialist will be assigned full-time to the Media Center. Alternative assignments will be agreed upon between the JSEP Principal and JSEP headquarters staff. MSDE will provide school library services at the smaller juvenile centers through a certified General Education Teacher or Instructional Assistant in collaboration with the MSDE JSEP Library Media Coordinator.

II. Library materials shall be selected by the JSEP Library Media Coordinator and Library Media Specialists according to the JSEP LMS Selection Policy (see attached copy.). The collection will consist of print and non-print materials, games, and other educational resources to support the school curriculum and the MSDE Library Media State Curriculum Standards. Questions regarding the appropriateness of any materials are to be referred to the school principal. The MSDE JSEP Library Media Coordinator and JSEP Director should be notified promptly. If the question can't be resolved at the school level, they should be referred to the MSDE JSEP Director and the MSDE JSEP Library Media Coordinator for review and resolution. Books or materials should not be removed from the library unless there is a clear and immediate security concern.

III. JSEP Library Media programs shall uniformly provide service to all youth on the basis of an established schedule as part of the regular school curriculum schedule. Every effort should be made to provide access to the Library Media Center each week. Access to Library Media Center services by youth on restrictive status shall be governed by the applicable JSEP school policies.

IV. Library Media Center materials and equipment are MSDE property and Library Media Center users as well as DJS and MSDE employees are responsible for their care and return.

V. Students violating Library Media Center policy may be denied access to the Media Center.

VI. The Library Media Center, equipment and furnishings shall not be used for other than Library Media Center purposes without prior consultation with and approval of the JSEP Principal. It is the responsibility of the DJS managing officer or facility administrator to maintain Library Media Center security outside school operating hours.

VII. Arrangements for Library Media services provided by outside agencies (county/public libraries, social agencies, cooperating partner agencies) or contractual employees will be made by the MSDE in cooperation with the DJS managing officer or facility administrator and principal. Specific procedures for the operation of Library Media services provided by outside agencies shall be developed by the JSEP Library Media Coordinator and JSEP school principal in cooperation with the DJS managing officer or facility administrator. Students shall be encouraged to utilize these services and shall be afforded access within established procedures.

VIII. Donation of Library Media Center materials or equipment shall be in accordance with the JSEP LMS Selection Policy (see attached copy). Donations of Library Media Center materials shall be coordinated through the MSDE JSEP Library Media Coordinator. Library Media Center donations are not to be accepted by DJS staff without prior consultation with the Library Media Coordinator.

IX. The DJS managing officer or facility administrator shall ensure that Library Media Center materials and equipment received at the school are safely delivered to the Library Media Center.

X. Each JSEP School Library Media Specialist will maintain the security of computer, telecommunications and presentation equipment in the Media Center. This equipment will be coded and given passwords to prevent unsupervised use. The Media Specialist, the JSEP School Principal, the Library Media Coordinator and MSDE IT Coordinator will have access to the passwords. Students must NOT have access to passwords. All Library Media Center computer equipment will be used under the direct supervision of the Media Specialist or Principal.

XI. Library Media Center materials will be purchased by the MSDE JSEP headquarters staff regardless of the source of funding. Schools providing supplemental funds for materials can specify the materials to be purchased based on local needs.

Nancy S. Grasmick
State Superintendent of Schools

200 West Baltimore Street • Baltimore, MD 21201 • 410-767-0100 • 410-333-6442 TTY/TDD

JSEP Library Media Materials Selection Policy – December, 2009

Prepared by: Roberta Reasoner, Library Media Coordinator, Juvenile Services Education Program
Maryland State Department of Education

Maryland State Department of Education (MSDE)
MISSION
The mission of the Maryland State Department of Education is to provide leadership, support, and accountability for effective systems of public education, library services and rehabilitation services.

Juvenile Services Education Program (JSEP)
MISSION
The program delivers a continuum of learning experiences to accelerate achievement, personal development, and readiness for a successful future.

VISION
The Juvenile Services Education Program will be recognized as a national leader in the education of detained and committed youth.

Juvenile Services Education Program Library Media Center Selection Policy Objectives:

I. The objective of the Library Media Center is to make available to faculty and students a collection of materials that will enrich and support the curriculum and meet the needs of the students and faculty served.

II. The main objective of the JSEP Library Media selection policy is to provide students with a wide range of educational materials on all levels of difficulty, offered in a variety of formats to take into consideration individual learning needs, abilities, and learning styles, with diversity of appeal and allowing for the presentation of many different points of view.

A. Materials in the library media center will provide:
   1. background information to supplement classroom instruction;
   2. a broad range of views on controversial issues to help students develop critical analytical skills;
   3. an appreciation of literature as a reflection of human experience and reading as a pleasurable activity; and
   4. appropriate print, non-print, and computer/online/digital resources in accordance and collaboration with the parameters of the MSDE.

Part 1: Procedures for Materials Selection

While selection of materials involves many people, including MSDE administrators, supervisors, teachers, library media specialists, and students, the responsibility for coordinating and recommending the selection and purchase of Library Media materials will rest with the JSEP Library Media Coordinator. Responsibility for coordinating the selection and purchase of textbooks is the responsibility of the JSEP Academic Coordinator. Other classroom materials may be purchased by the site-based administrator.

The Library Media Center provides media in a wide variety of fields including the sciences, arts, and the humanities. The following factors will be considered important in the implementation of the library's goal.

1. Support of the instructional curriculum of the school.
2. Groups or individual's needs and interests existing in the youth population, such as those relating to age, ethnic origin, and gender.
3. Provide for individual learning needs, abilities, and learning styles.
4. Flexibility to meet and satisfy new and changing social interests and needs.
5. Priorities established because of budget limitations and requirements of funding sources (see individual programs).

At all times, the material's excellence (artistic, literary, etc.), appropriateness to level of user, superiority in treatment of controversial issues, and ability to stimulate further intellectual and social development will be considered as part of the purchasing decision. Materials shall be recommended for purchase based on continuous assessment by the on-site Media Specialist with the aid of professional tools. Recommendations will be sent to the JSEP Library Media Coordinator for final approval and centralized purchasing.

Staff members involved in selection of Library Media Center materials shall use the following criteria as a guide:

1. educational significance
2. contribution the subject matter makes to the curriculum and to the interests of the students
3. favorable reviews found in standard selection sources
4. favorable recommendations based on preview and examination of materials by professional personnel
5. reputation and significance of the author, producer, and publisher
6. validity, currency, and appropriates of material
7. contribution the material makes to breadth of representative viewpoints on controversial issues
8. high degree of potential user appeal
9. high artistic quality and/or literary style
10. quality and variety of format
11. value commensurate with cost and/or need
12. timeliness or permanence
13. integrity

The following recommended lists shall be consulted in the selection of materials, but selection is not limited to their listings:
Bibliographies (latest editions available, including supplements)

1. *American Historical Fiction*
2. *American Library Association booklists, including, but not limited to:*
   • Best Books for Young Adults
   • Booklist's Editors Choice – Adult Books for Young Adults
   • Best Graphic Novels for Young Adults
   • Michael L. Printz Award for excellence in Young Adult Literature
   • Popular Paperbacks for Young Adults
   • Quick Picks for Reluctant Young Adult Readers
   • Teens' Top Ten Books
3. *European Historical Fiction and Biography*
4. *Middle and Junior High Core Collection*
5. *Subject Guide to Children's Books in Print*
6. *Subject Index to Books for Intermediate Grades*

Current reviewing media:

1. *AASA Science Books and Films*
2. *American Film & Video Association Evaluations*
3. *Booklist*
4. *Library Media Connection*
5. *School Library Journal*
6. *Teen Urban Fiction*

Materials will be selected for the Library Media Center that are:

1. integral to the instructional program.
2. appropriate for the reading level and understanding of students in the school.
3. reflecting the interests and needs of the students and faculty served by the library media center.
4. presenting a variety of formats to support different learning styles.
5. warranting inclusion in the collection because of their literary and/or artistic value and merit.
6. stimulating the students' higher-order thinking and creativity skills.
7. presenting information with the greatest degree of accuracy and clarity possible.
8. representing a fair and unbiased presentation of information. In controversial areas, the Media Specialist, in cooperation with the faculty, should select materials representing as many opinions as possible, in order that varying viewpoints are available to students.

Due to the nature of the student population and the instructional program, MSDE JSEP staff will not distribute any publication or materials determined to be detrimental to the security, good order, or discipline of the Juvenile Services Education Program in the schools. Publications which may not be distributed include but are not limited to those which meet one of the following criteria: (a) they depict or describe procedures for the construction or use of weapons, ammunition, bombs or incendiary devices; (b) they depict or describe methods of escape from correctional facilities, or contains blueprints, drawings or similar descriptions of the same; (c) they depict or describe procedures for the brewing or manufacture of alcoholic beverages or drugs; (d) they are written in code; (e) they encourage or instruct in the commission of criminal activity; (f) they contain sexually explicit material which by its nature or content poses a threat to the security, good order, or discipline of the school; (g) they contain homophobic, pornographic, obscene or sexually explicit material or other visual depictions that are inappropriate to students; (h) they use language or images that are inappropriate in the education setting or disruptive to the educational process; (i) they contain information or materials that could cause damage or danger of disruption to the educational process; (j) they depict, describe or encourage activities , language or images that advocate violence or discrimination toward other people (e.g., hate literature) or that may constitute harassment or discrimination or create a serious danger of violence in the facility; and (k) materials depicting the practice of tattooing.

The following criteria will be used as they apply to the Library Media Center materials:

1. Materials will support and be consistent with the general educational goals of the state and the aims and objectives of individual schools and specific courses.
2. Materials will meet high standards of quality in factual content and presentation.
3. Materials will be appropriate for the subject area and for the age, emotional development, ability level, learning styles, and social development of the students for whom the materials are selected.
4. Physical format and appearance of materials will be suitable for their intended use.
5. Materials will be designed to help students gain an awareness of our pluralistic society.
6. Materials will be designed to motivate students and staff to examine their own duties, responsibilities, rights, and privileges as participating citizens in our society, and to make informed judgments in their daily lives.
7. Materials will be selected for their strengths rather than rejected for their weaknesses.
8. The selection of materials on controversial issues will be directed toward maintaining a diverse collection representing various views.
9. Materials will clarify historical and contemporary forces by presenting and analyzing intergroup tension and conflict objectively, placing emphasis on recognizing and understanding social and economic problems.

Procedures for selecting Library Media Center materials include:

1. In selecting materials, professional personnel will evaluate available resources and curriculum needs and will consult reputable, professionally prepared aids to selection, and other appropriate sources. The actual resource will be examined whenever possible.
2. Recommendations for purchase involve administrators, teachers, students, DJS personnel, and community partners/persons, as appropriate.
3. Gift materials will be judged and accepted or rejected by the selection criteria.
4. Selection is an ongoing process that will include how to remove materials no longer appropriate and how to replace lost and worn materials still of educational value.
5. Requests, suggestions, and reactions for the purchase of instructional materials will be gathered from staff to the greatest extent possible and students when appropriate.

6. Reviews of proposed acquisitions will be sought in the literature of reputable professional organizations and other reviewing sources recognized for their objectivity and wide experience.
7. Materials will be examined by professional staff to the extent necessary or to apply criteria.
8. School Media Center materials selection will be coordinated by the MSDE certified Media Specialist, or the MSDE JSEP Library Media Coordinator, where there is no professional staff, and involve teachers and curriculum specialists. Recommendations will be sent to the MSDE Library Media Coordinator for final approval and centralized purchasing.
9. Professionally recognized reviewing periodicals, standard catalogs, and other selection aids are used by the Media Specialists and the faculty to guide them in their selection.

Part 2: Procedures for Dealing with Challenged Materials
Occasional objections to instructional materials will be made despite the quality of the selection process; therefore, the procedure for handling reconsideration of challenged materials in response to questions concerning their appropriateness is outlined herein. This procedure establishes the framework for registering a complaint appropriate action while defending the principles of freedom of information, the students' right to access of materials, and the professional responsibility and integrity of the school faculty and administration.

The principles of intellectual freedom are inherent in the First Amendment to the Constitution of the United States and are expressed in the *Library Bill of Rights*, adopted by the Council of the American Library Association. If instructional materials are questioned, the principles of intellectual freedom should be defended rather than the materials.

The MSDE JSEP subscribes in principle to the statements of policy on intellectual freedom and library philosophy as expressed in the text of the **First Amendment** to the United States Constitution—"Congress shall make no law respecting an establishment of religion, or prohibiting the free exercise thereof; or abridging the freedom of speech, or of the press; or the right of the people peaceable to assemble, and to petition the Government for a redress of grievances," and to the American Library Association's ***Library Bill of Rights*** (see Appendix I).

Reconsideration procedure:
No duly selected materials whose appropriateness is challenged shall be removed from the school except upon the recommendation of a **reconsideration committee**, with the concurrence of the MSDE JSEP Director, or upon the MSDE JSEP Director's recommendation, the concurrence of the State Superintendent or, upon the State Superintendent's recommendation, the concurrence of the State Board of Education, or upon formal action of the State Board of Education when a recommendation of a reconsideration committee is appealed to it.

Procedures to be observed:

1. All complaints to the Media Specialist shall be reported to the JSEP school principal involved, whether received by telephone, letter, or in personal conversation.

2. The JSEP principal shall contact the complainant to discuss the challenge and attempt to resolve it informally by explaining the mission and goals of the school and/or the Library Media Center; shall explain to the questioner the school's selection procedure, criteria, and qualifications of those persons selecting the resource; and shall explain the particular place the material occupies in the education program, its intended educational usefulness, and additional information regarding its use, or refer the party to someone who can identify and explain the use of the resource.

3. After informal negotiation, if the challenge is not resolved informally, the complainant shall receive a **Letter to Complainant upon receipt of challenge (see Appendix II)** from the JSEP principal and shall be supplied with a packet of materials consisting of the JSEP Library Media Services instructional goals and objectives, materials selection policy statement, and the procedure for handling objections. This packet also will include a standard printed form, the **Request for Reconsideration of Library Media Center Resources, (see Appendix III)** which shall be completed and returned before consideration will be given to the complaint.

4. If the formal request for reconsideration has not been received by the JSEP principal within two weeks, it shall be considered closed. If the request is returned, the reasons for selection of the specific work shall be reestablished by the appropriate staff.

5. Access to challenged material shall not be restricted during the reconsideration process. Pending the outcome of the request for reconsideration, however, access to questioned materials can be denied to the student (s) of the parent/guardian making the complaint, if they so desire.

6. Upon receipt of a completed objection form, the JSEP principal involved will convene a committee of five to consider the complaint. This committee shall consist of the MSDE Library Media Coordinator, the MSDE Academic Coordinator, and these people from the school involved: the principal, the Library Media Specialist and a teacher. If possible, a student and/or parent may also be selected to serve on the committee.

7. The committee shall meet to discuss the materials, following the guidelines set forth in the **Instructions to Reconsideration Committee**, (see Appendix IV) and shall prepare a report on the material containing its recommendations on disposition of the matter.

   A. The reconsideration committee shall:
      1. Read and/or view the challenged resource;
      2. Determine professional acceptance by reading critical reviews of the resource;
      3. Weigh values and faults and form opinions based on the material as a whole rather than on passages or sections taken out of context;
      4. Discuss the challenged resource in the context of the educational program;
      5. Discuss the challenged item with the individual questioner when appropriate;
      6. Prepare a written report.

   B. The written report shall be discussed with the individual complainant if requested.

   C. The written report shall be retained by the school principal, with copies forwarded to the MSDE JSEP Director and MSDE Library Media Coordinator. A minority report also may be filed.

   D. Written reports, once filed, are confidential and available for examination by appropriate officials only.

   E. The decision of the reconsideration committee is binding for the individual school.

8. The JSEP principal shall notify complainant of the decision and send a formal report and recommendation to the MSDE JSEP Director. In answering the complainant, the JSEP principal shall explain the book selection policy and procedure, give the guidelines used for

selection, and cite authorities used in reaching decisions. If the committee decides to keep the work that caused the complaint, the complainant shall be given an explanation. If the complaint is valid, the JSEP principal will acknowledge it and make recommended changes.

9. Notwithstanding any procedure outlined in this policy, the questioner shall have the right to appeal any decision of the reconsideration committee to the State Board of Education as the final review panel.

10. If the complainant is still not satisfied, he or she may ask the MSDE JSEP Director to present an appeal to the State Superintendent and the Board of Education, which shall make a final determination of the issue. The Board of Education may seek assistance from outside organizations such as the American Library Association, the Association for Supervision and Curriculum Development, etc., in making its determination.

Guiding Principles for Process

1. Any resident or employee of the school may raise objection to materials used in a school's educational program, despite the fact that the individuals selecting such resources were duly qualified to make the selection, followed the proper procedure, and observed the criteria for selecting learning resources.

2. The principal should review the selection and reconsideration policy and procedures with the teaching staff at least annually.

3. No parent/guardian has the right to determine reading, viewing, or listening matter for students other than his or her own children.

4. The MSDE JSEP supports the *Library Bill of Rights*, adopted by the American Library Association (see Appendix I). When learning resources are challenged, the principles of the freedom to read/listen/view must be defended as well.

5. Access to challenged material shall not be restricted during the reconsideration process.

6. The major criterion for the final decision is the appropriateness of the material for its intended educational use.

7. A decision to sustain a challenge shall not necessarily be interpreted as a judgment of irresponsibility by the professionals involved in the original selection and/or use of the material.

Appendix I: Library Bill of Rights

Library Bill of Rights

The American Library Association affirms that all libraries are forums for information and ideas, and that the following basic policies should guide their services.

I. Books and other library resources should be provided for the interest, information, and enlightenment of all people of the community the library serves. Materials should not be excluded because of the origin, background, or views of those contributing to their creation.

II. Libraries should provide materials and information presenting all points of view on current and historical issues. Materials should not be proscribed or removed because of partisan or doctrinal disapproval.

III. Libraries should challenge censorship in the fulfillment of their responsibility to provide information and enlightenment.

IV. Libraries should cooperate with all persons and groups concerned with resisting abridgment of free expression and free access to ideas.

V. A person's right to use a library should not be denied or abridged because of origin, age, background, or views.

VI. Libraries which make exhibit spaces and meeting rooms available to the public they serve should make such facilities available on an equitable basis, regardless of the beliefs or affiliations of individuals or groups requesting their use.

Adopted June 19, 1939, by the ALA Council; amended October 14, 1944; June 18, 1948; February 2, 1961; June 27, 1967; January 23, 1980; inclusion of "age" reaffirmed January 23, 1996.

"Library Bill of Rights," American Library Association, June 30, 2006.http://www.ala.org/ala/aboutala/offices/oif/statementspols/statementsif/librarybillrights.cfm (Accessed December 28, 2009) Document ID: 24930

Nancy S. Grasmick
State Superintendent of Schools

200 West Baltimore Street • Baltimore, MD 21201 • 410-767-0100 • 410-333-6442 TTY/TDD

Appendix II: Letter to Complainant upon receipt of challenge:

Dear:

We appreciate your concern over the use of _____ in our school. The school has developed procedures for selecting materials, but realizes that not everyone will agree with every selection made.

To help you understand the selection process, we are sending copies of the JSEP Library Media Services:

1. Instructional goals and objectives
2. Materials Selection Policy statement
3. Procedure for Handling Objections

If you are still concerned after you review this material, please complete the Request for Reconsideration of Material form and return it to me. You may be assured of prompt attention to your request. If I have not heard from you within two weeks, we will assume you no longer wish to file a formal complaint.

Sincerely,

Principal

Nancy S. Grasmick
State Superintendent of Schools

200 West Baltimore Street • Baltimore, MD 21201 • 410-767-0100 • 410-333-6442 TTY/TDD

Appendix III: Request for Reconsideration of Library Media Center Resources

The Maryland State Department of Education Juvenile Services Education Program has delegated the responsibility for selection and evaluation of library/educational resources to the JSEP Library Media Coordinator and the school library media specialist/curriculum committee, and has established reconsideration procedures to address concerns about those resources. Completion of this form is the first step in those procedures. If you wish to request reconsideration of school or library resources, please return the completed form to:

Library Media Coordinator, Juvenile Services Education Program, Maryland State Department of Education, 200 West Baltimore Street, Baltimore, MD 21201-2595

Name _____Date _____

Address _____

City _____State _____Zip _____

Phone (Home/Work) _____Phone (Cell)_____

Do you represent self? _____ Organization? _____

1. Resource on which you are commenting:
____ Book ____ Textbook ____ Video ____ Display____ Magazine ____ Library Program

____ Audio Recording____ Newspaper ____ Electronic information/network (please specify)

____ Other _____

Title _____

Author/Producer _____

2. What brought this resource to your attention?
3. Have you read and/or viewed the entire resource?
4. What concerns you about the resource? (use other side or additional pages if necessary)
5. Are there resource(s) you suggest to provide additional information and/or other viewpoints on this topic?

Nancy S. Grasmick
State Superintendent of Schools

200 West Baltimore Street • Baltimore, MD 21201 • 410-767-0100 • 410-333-6442 TTY/TDD

Appendix IV: Instructions to Reconsideration Committee

Bear in mind the principles of the **freedom to learn and to read** and base your decision on these broad principles rather than on defense of individual materials. Freedom of inquiry is vital to education in a democracy.

Study thoroughly all materials referred to you and read available reviews. The general acceptance of the materials should be checked by consulting standard evaluation aids and local holdings in other schools.

Passages or parts should not be pulled out of context. The values and faults should be weighed against each other and the opinions based on the materials as a whole.

Your report, presenting both majority and minority opinions, will be presented by the principal to the complainant at the conclusion of your discussion of the questioned material.

Hennepin County Library @ Juvenile Dentention Center(JDC)	
WHAT IS IT?	The Library provides a collection of books, magazines, and comic books of interest to JDC students.
WHERE IS THE LIBRARY?	The Library is located in the gym. During the school year, library staff visit each classroom to provide library service.
WHEN IS IT OPEN?	Library staff visit JDC on the 2nd and 4th Thursday of each month. JDC staff may also visit the library with residents at other times, but should ensure that rules using the library are followed and the library is left in good condition.
HOW MANY ITEMS MAY RESIDENTS HAVE?	**Students are limited to five items from the library.**
WHERE DO YOU RETURN BOOKS?	Books should be returned in the resident's mod. JDC staff will gather materials on a regular basis and return them to the library. No library materials may leave the facility.
WHAT BOOKS ARE THERE?	The library has over 2,000 books. They are a mix of fiction and nonfiction in both hardback and paperback.
WHAT MAGAZINES?	Magazines include *Slam, Vibe, Right On, Dub*, and other materials of interest to residents as permitted by JDC staff
WHAT SUBJECTS?	In non-fiction, JDC students will find books in the areas of: Sports, Health, Poetry, Math/Science, History, Urban Studies, Religion, and Art. There are also sections of books on Latino, Native American, and Afro-American studies. There is also a large section of graphic novels and comic books.
WHAT AUTHORS?	There is fiction, in paperback and hardback, available from most major authors, such as Stephen King, Dean Koontz, J.K. Rowling, Omar Tyree, Eric Jerome Dickey, Gary Paulsen, Walter Dean Myers, John Sandford, Sidney Sheldon, James Patterson, and Sister Souljah.
WHAT IS NOT HERE?	The library will **not** provide items which present a threat to the security of the JDC or materials which have been deemed inappropriate by JDC administration. Such items include books with graphic sexual content, gang content, or graphic violence.
CAN RESIDNETS RESERVE A BOOK?	Yes. If resident wish to read a certain book, they may request it. Staff should email _____or call (952-847-8859) with the name of book, the author if known, and the resident's name/ mod. Library staff will distribute reserve at the next visit.
MORE QUESTIONS?	_____ will be happy to answer any questions, take suggestions for books, or hear your comments about the library.

AGREEMENT BETWEEN HENNEPIN COUNTY LIBRARY AND
HENNEPIN COUNTY JUVENILE DETENTION CENTER

Hennepin County Library through this agreement provides library services to the Hennepin County Juvenile Detention Center. Hennepin County Library Board Policy on *SERVICES TO GROUPS & INDIVIDUALS WITH RESTRICTED LIBRARY ACCESS* addresses provision of services to populations who are unable to travel to the Library, including those in detention facilities. The Library's Outreach Section is responsible for working with the Juvenile Detention Center staff to assure access to library materials and services for Center residents, in accordance with the policies and procedures established by the Library and the Center. Both the Library and the Juvenile Detention Center recognize the educational and recreational needs of library users in institutional settings, as well as the residents' right to information.

This agreement is to run from July 1, 2009, through June 30, 2010.

Services:

1. Juvenile Detention Center will provide funding in the amount of $2,300 for the time of this agreement for the purchase of paperbacks and magazines for the Center deposit collection. The money will be transferred to the Library through a County fund transfer.
2. Deposit collections maintained in the Juvenile Detention Center include regularly purchased paperbacks and periodicals that are in accordance with collection selection criteria. Donated materials may be included when they meet collection selection criteria.
3. Library staff will visit the Juvenile Detention Center twice each month to maintain the deposit collection and to assist residents in requesting specific materials or information on specific subjects.

Policies controlling this agreement:

1. Materials provided to fill specific requests by residents are selected in accordance with the Hennepin County Library Collection Management Policy, if they do not represent a threat to the security of the Juvenile Detention Center.
2. HCL recognizes that under the county 's policy regarding residental housing units (RH-102) that JDC has "the duty to ensure that its residents choose appropirate reading material."
3. Library staff will select the materials to be provided to the Juvenile Detention Center. Library staff, in consultation with JDC staff, will develop and utilize a collection plan which supports adolescent literacy and is geared to their reading interests and levels and English language abilities.
4. Library materials are placed in the Juvenile Detention Center library area to guarantee free and open access for all residents.
5. Materials currently supplied are of a general informational and recreational nature. Staff training materials and materials for formal education programs, including textbooks, generally are not supplied through the deposit collection.
6. Juvenile Detention Center staff may request in writing that a specific item be removed from the collection. (see below) These requests must cite specific objections to the work being

housed at the Center. The requests will be reviewed and decisions as delineated in the procedures below.

7. Library materials at the Juvenile Detention Center are placed there for use by residents of the institution. They may not be taken from the institution by staff or residents.

PROCEDURES

1. If staff or residents of the Juvenile Detention Center object to material supplied by the Library, JDC still will communicate the specific objections to the material, citing pages if necessary using a request for reconsideration form (see attached). This completed form and the book/material should be sent to Correction Unit Supervisor who will have the material removed pending a meeting with the Outreach Supervisor to discuss the complaint. When a decision is reached, the complainant will be informed. If dissatisfied, the complainant may appeal the decision of the Correction Unit Supervisor to the Superintendent. In the event the Superintendent and the Outreach Supervisor are unable to agree, the Juvenile Detention Center Superintendent will be the final authority.

2. Residents are encouraged to return books to the library as soon as they have finished reading them to make them available to others.

3. All books/materials which have been borrowed from the library's general collection in response to a special request and must be returned to Hennepin County Library staff during their regular visits.

4. Staff from the Hennepin County Library Outreach Section visit twice a month. During this time, library staff will
   a. Take requests for materials from the residents.
   b. Put out, promote, and circulate materials.
   c. Interact with residents and inquire regarding their reading interests
   d. Weed the collection as to its physical condition and content. Books are removed and discarded if they are worn and in poor condition, or if there is no longer interest in the particular title.

5. Both HCL and JDC Staff will, in providing library services, demonstrate the core competencies expected of all county employees in the areas of customer focus, integrity and trust, supporting vision and purpose, building relationships, resiliency, and technical knowledge.

6. Staff of the JDC and HCL will work together to make the library an enriching aspect of a resident's stay at JDC. JDC staff will ensure that all residents have the opportunity to visit the library during the times when library staff make scheduled visits.

7. While residents are allowed to use the JDC Library on days when Library staff is not available, it is the responsibly of JDC staff to ensure the library and the materials are treated with respect.

The following Library Staff acknowledge their responsibilities for implementing and managing this agreement.

_____

Manager, Outreach Services   Date

_____

Youth Services Coordinator, Hennepin County Library   Date

_____

The following Detention Staff acknowledge their responsibilities for implementing and managing this agreement.

Name	Position Title	Date
Name	Position Title	Date
Name	Position Title	Date
Name	Position Title	Date

Request for Reconsideration of materials at Juvenile Detention Center
Author: _____
Title: _____
How does this item present a threat to the security of the institution and/or does not represent choose appropriate reading material." Please be specific, citing pages if possible.

_____
_____
_____
_____
_____
_____
_____
_____
_____
_____
_____

Name: _____
Mod: _____
Phone: _____
Email: _____

HENNEPIN COUNTY LIBRARY AND INTERMEDIATE DISTRICT 287 LIBRARY AGREEMENT

This Agreement is made and entered into by and between the Hennepin County Library, hereinafter referred to as "HCL", and Intermediate District 287's educational program located at the Hennepin County Home School, hereinafter referred to as "Epsilon". The Hennepin County Library extends library service to residents of Hennepin County Home School (HCHS) in acknowledgment of their restricted access to public libraries. In providing this service, it is recognized that the informational and recreational needs of residents in institutional settings that are balanced against the facility's overall objectives regarding treatment and security. This Agreement covers only those library services provided directly to the Epsilon program. A separate agreement is signed between the Hennepin County Library (HCL) and Department of Community Corrections (DCC).

POLICIES

1. This Agreement shall be in force and effect from July 1, 2009, through June 30, 2011.
2. The Outreach Section of Hennepin County Library (HCL) will be responsible for providing library services to the Epsilon program. Outreach Manager, Patrick Jones will be the staff contact for the Library branch located at the HCHS. Jody Delau, Administrative Intern, will be the primary administrative contact for the Epsilon program.
3. The scope of the collection will restrict only those materials that present a threat to the security of the institution and/or the advancement of treatment programs. Specific titles/subjects have been identified as restricted, and a process designed for staff to request additional items be removed from the library collection. (See Attachment A.)
4. Materials selected and provided to the Epsilon program as part of the HCL collection shall meet the cultural, informational, educational and recreational needs of the residents. Materials selected will be based upon a collection development plan completed by the HCL in cooperation with HCHS and Epsilon staff.
5. Library cards used to check out materials will have a fine free status. Overdue notices will be sent for unreturned materials. There will be no charge to Epsilon for damaged or lost materials, but Epsilon staff will make every effort to see that library materials are returned and in satisfactory condition.

SERVICES

1. The Outreach Section will maintain a branch library at the HCHS. All books, fixtures, and posters are property of the HCL. Outreach staff will visit the HCL on a monthly basis to add new materials, purge older materials as appropriate, and obtain requests from HCHS residents. HCHS staff and Epsilon staff will work with the Outreach Section to develop a schedule of visits so that HCHS residents have ample access to the library.
2. HCL will deliver requested materials to the HCHS administration building once a week. Epsilon staff will distribute these materials to the students. The returned books will be boxed, labeled "Return to OS" and placed on the administration building loading dock for weekly pickup.

3. HCL staff will provide regular booktalks for English classes and supply multiple copies of requested titles. Language arts teachers may also request other titles for students at any time by email to the HCL Outreach Manager.
4. At least one time during the year, representatives from the HCL will meet with HCHS and Epsilon Program Administrator or designee to evaluate library services.
5. If funding is available, school year programs such as author visits, creative writing workshops, publication of a literary magazine, etc will be developed by the HCL in conjunction with Epsilon program administrative staff.
6. The language arts teacher(s) will be primary staff requesting materials from residents.

OTHER

1. Modifications to the terms and conditions of this Agreement may be made during the contract term subject to prior approval of the parties.

For the Hennepin County Library   For the Epsilon Program / District 287

_____   _____

Outreach Manager   Administrative Intern

_____   _____

Hennepin County Library   Program Supervisor

HENNEPIN COUNTY HOME SCHOOL RESTRICTED MATERIALS

1. The scope of the collection will restrict only those materials that present a threat to the security of the institution and/or the advancement of treatment programs. The materials listed below have been deemed by HCL staff as a threat to security or interfering with the advancement of treatment programs, and thus will not be brought onto the campus by HCL staff, by volunteers engaged by the HCHS, or by family members of HCHS residents.

2. The responsibility of monitoring the materials referenced herein primarily rests with HCHS staff. However, HCL and Epsilon staff is expected to be vigilant in ensuring that such materials are not allowed into the school or other areas of the facility.

3. If HCHS staff wishes to have materials prohibited for all residents, they should fill out the appropriate form and send to _____, Administrative Intern. The reconsideration form will be sent to _____ at the library who will gather information about the materials in question. He will convene a meeting of a representative from Epsilon and DCC. This group of three will decide if the material should be retained or removed from HCHS. Materials will only be restricted upon completion of the Request for Reconsideration form process.

4. HCL staff will not distribute any publication or materials determined to be detrimental to the security, good order, or discipline of the HCHS. Publications which may not be distributed include but are not limited to those which meet one of the following criteria: (a) they depict or describe procedures for the construction or use of weapons, ammunition, bombs or incendiary devices; (b) they depict, encourage, or describe methods of escape from correctional facilities, or contains blueprints, drawings or similar descriptions of the same; (c) they depict or describe procedures for the brewing of alcoholic beverages, or the manufacture of drugs; (d) they are written in code; (e) they depict, describe or encourage activities which may lead to the use of physical violence or group disruption; (f) they encourage or instruct in the commission of criminal activity; (g) they contain sexually explicit material which by its nature or content pose a threat to the security, good order, or discipline of the HCHS; (h) homophobic, pornographic, obscene or sexually explicit material or other visual depictions that are harmful to students; (i) materials that use obscene, abusive, profane, lewd, vulgar, rude, inflammatory, threatening, disrespectful, or sexually explicit language; (j) materials that use language or images that are inappropriate in the education setting or disruptive to the educational process; (k) information or materials that could cause damage or danger of disruption to the educational process; (l) materials that use language or images that advocate violence or discrimination toward other people (hate literature) or that may constitute harassment or discrimination or create a serious danger of violence in the facility; (m) materials depicting martial arts; and (n) materials depicting tattooing.

5. Books and materials requested that are not on the approved list, or have not been previously barred by the HCL, will be reviewed on a case-by-case basis prior to being distributed to residents of the HCHS.

6. Residents in Cottage 3 may receive comic books on the approved reading list. Residents in TLC and cottage 2 may receive magazines that are on the approved reading list. Residents in Cottage 4 are prohibited from any magazine with heavy sexual or violent content, and any book featuring murder, rape, or overt sexual content. Residents in Cottages 6 may not receive comic books or magazines.

Request for Reconsideration of materials at Hennepin County Home School

Author: _____

Title: _____

How does this item present a threat to the security of the institution and/or the advancement of treatment program? Please be specific, citing pages or passages if possible.

_____
_____
_____
_____
_____
_____
_____
_____
_____
_____
_____
_____
_____
_____
_____
_____
_____
_____
_____
_____

Name: _____
Cottage#: _____
Phone: _____
Email: _____

Please send to Administrative Intern

Please note that materials that are considered a threat to security or the advancement of treatment programs are not to be permitted in any area of the Hennepin County Home School.

Hennepin County Library / Epsilon program 2009–2010 school year plan

The Hennepin County Library offers its award-winning Great Transitions to the Hennepin County Home School as collaboration between District 287, Hennepin County Community Corrections, and the Outreach Department of the Library.

Great Transitions provides intensive, participatory literacy and library-related programming for students during their incarceration at the Hennepin County Home School. Surveys from residents indicate increased amounts of reading, improved attitudes about reading, and better self-concept as readers as a results of Great Transitions. CHS administration contend that a strong literacy-based library program can play a role in reducing recidivism among residents.

Activity	Description	Frequency	Comment
Student book requests	Students may request books through their Language Arts teachers. These requests are given to an educational assistant who then contacts the Library. Every Thursday, the Library ships requested books to CHS to be distributed to students. The Library will not send any books which CHS and Epsilon staff believe present a threat to the security of the institution and/or the advancement of treatment programs. If CHS and Epsilon staff object to materials sent by the library, there is a reconsideration process for them to follow.	Ongoing, starting September 8	For 2008 - 2009 school year, there will **two significant changes**. Books for students in Cottage 4 will be given to County staff who will distribute / monitor book requests. **Epsilon and CHS staff will work out details on this arrangement.** As an experiment, girls in cottage two will be given library cards. Books will come to the school checked out to individuals, not the institution. Details to follow. **Thus, Epsilon staff will no longer need to monitor materials given to residents in Cottage 2 and 4.**
Diverse City	The Library publishes an annual literary magazine entitled Diverse City. Students submit up writing and art for publication, which is vetted by CHS for inappropriate content. The finished publication is distributed widely, with student authors receiving multiplies copies, as well as copies for other students, CHS staff, Epsilon staff, and other stakeholders.	To be determined, but no later than spring 2010	Library staff will work with Language Arts teachers to determine best times within school year to do workshops. The library does not have funding to provide someone to teacher a creative writing workshop as in the past. It will depend upon the Language Arts and Fine Arts teachers to recruit works for the publication.
TLC	As part of the TLC program, each student goes the HCL Central Library where they receive a new library card, a waiver for any old library fines, a tour of the building, and fill out a survey.	Ongoing, starting July 2009	

Activity	Description	Frequency	Comment
Library @ CHS	The Outreach Department maintains a library on site at the CHS. The library has over 5,000 books that are a mix of fiction and nonfiction. Library staff visit CHS once a month during the school day as part of Language Arts classes. This is a book only collection; magazines are delivered to each CHS cottage from the library on a monthly basis. The Library will not contain any books which CHS and Epsilon staff are inappropriate. If CHS and Epsilon staff object to materials housed in the library, there is a reconsideration process for them to follow	Monthly, beginning September 18	**Dates for 2008 are** ☆ Sept 18 ☆ Oct 16 ☆ Nov 20 ☆ Dec 18 **Dates for 2009 are** ☆ January 15 ☆ February 19 ☆ March 19 ☆ April 16 ☆ May 21 ☆ June 18
Booktalks	Booktalks are short advertisements for books of interest to students. Librarians schedule the visits directly with one of the Language Arts teachers and then talk titles from a list during one school day. Residents request titles from the booktalks, which are then delivered to the school to distribute to students.	Monthly, beginning **October** 2008	First date will in October. Booktalkers will work with _____ to schedule visit
Other support	Teachers may request materials (books, DVDs, audio books) to support their instruction directly from the library. The library can often provide classroom sets of titles. The library can also provide on using the Library's Teen Links	As needed	

(continued)

Activity	Description	Frequency	Comment
	electronic resources to find information on the library's web site, although students do not have Internet access normally to directly apply the teaching.		
Cottage collections	The Library sends to cottages a monthly collection of new materials; some cottages at do not receive magazines.	Monthly and ongoing	

Collection Development Policy
Platte Valley Youth Service Center Library
Revised July 2008

I. **Introduction**

The purpose of the Platte Valley Youth Services Center (PVYSC) Library is to provide a wide range of diverse reading and instructional materials for students, teachers, and staff. This policy will be reviewed annually and updated by the media specialist as necessary. PVYSC supports and adheres to the Freedom to Read Statement of the American Library Association, the American Library Association Bill of Rights and the American Library Association's Resolution on Prisoners' Right to Read (see Appendix A). PVYSC also supports the Division of Youth Corrections Policy 17.9 on Library Services (see Appendix B).

II. **Collection Management and Development Policies**

A. Clientele

The clientele to be served by the PCYSC library include students, teachers, and PCYSC staff, including counselors, administrators, and security staff. Due to the nature of this facility, materials will not be readily available to the community. Teachers and PCYSC staff will have access to all materials (i.e. films, books, periodicals, etc), however students will be able to check out books only.

B. Subject Boundaries

General subject boundaries will include materials that support the curriculum and the interests of the students.

C. Priorities and Limitations governing selection

1. Materials for the library will come from the following sources: the PCYSC library budget, the Department of Institutions at the Colorado Department of Education, grants, and gifts or donations.

2. Forms of materials to be collected include books, VHS and DVD films, and magazines.

3. Materials in the collection will be primarily in the English language; however, a small and relevant Spanish Language selection will be maintained. The media specialist will access materials in other languages as necessary from outside sources through the use of inner library loan.

4. This library shall exclude materials that glorify criminal behavior. Nonfiction materials on the subject of crime/criminology shall be fact based and purchased for their historical significance and/or the support of the school curriculum.

5. Due to the small size of the student population, duplicate materials will not routinely be purchased without special request.

6. This library shall participate in the School District 6 inner library loan program. Either the media specialist or teachers may obtain items. The person requesting the item is responsible for its return, as well as for the payment of any lost or damaged items.

7. Application to the LSCA grant shall be considered on an annual basis and such application must be approved by the school administrator.

8. Progress in the collections development, library programs, and changes in policies and procedures may be reported quarterly in the state report submitted by the PCYSC school.

9. Gifts/donations of books will be added to the collection only after a careful physical examination has been made to check for both contraband and content in

relation to selection policy criteria. Materials not selected or used will be either distributed to pods or disposed of as appropriate.

10. While this library will provide Internet access to students, this institution reserves the right to restrict the use of the Internet based on:
    a. The Internet contract signed by each student
    b. The teachers' and staffs' best professional judgment

III. **Selection Policy**

PCYSC will adhere to the School District Six Materials Selection Procedure (see appendix C) and the following guidelines:

A. Responsibility for selection and de-selection of materials shall rest with the media specialist who will follow criteria set forth by the Board of Education, the administration of PCYSC, and this policy. Suggestions for selection will be welcomed from students, teachers, and PVYSC staff.

B. Selection criteria will be based on Teacher and Student needs as well as budget constraints.

1. General criteria for materials shall include:
   a. relevancy to today's world
   b. representation of artistic, historic, and literary qualities
   c. reflection of the problems/aspirations, attitudes, and ideals of various societies
   d. contribution to the objectives of the instructional program and curriculum
   e. consistency with and support of the district and state standards and goals
   f. appropriateness for the age and ability level and social and emotional development of the users
   g. ability to meet quality standards in terms of content, format, and presentation
   h. helpfulness in gaining an awareness of a diverse and multicultural society
   i. motivation of students to examine their own attitudes, right, and responsibilities as citizens and makes informed judgments in their daily lives
   j. selection for strengths rather than rejected for weaknesses
   k. requests from library users
   l. currency and appropriateness of the materials
   m. high degree of potential user appeal
   n. no presentation of a personal bias

2. Specific criteria for materials shall include:
   a. fiction books shall be purchased based on their literary merit and student interest. Selection decisions will be made under the consideration that PCYSC residents to not have the opportunity to independently seek out other sources for books.
   b. nonprint materials will be selected based on instruction/curriculum needs. The selection and use of films will be based on District 6 Policy 6600 *Use of Motion Pictures in the Classroom* (see appendix D).
   c. a portion of each year's budget shall be used to support multicultural materials
   d. a variety of selection aids will e consulted and used based on needs at the time of selection
   e. periodicals shall be selected based on:
      i. approval by PCYSC administration
      ii. student and teacher requests
      iii. the amount of money allocated by CDE's Department of Institutions

C. The policy for de-selection follows the same criteria for selection

1. Staff or students wishing to challenge a holding in the PVYSC library shall adhere to the procedures laid out in section VI of this document
2. Requests to remove material from the collection made by the director of PCYSC will be honored immediately

IV. **Policies for Acquisition**
   A. Materials shall be acquired through the most efficient source, based on cost effectiveness and time constraints. Processing for the books shall be purchased whenever possible.

V. **Evaluation of the Collection**
   A. Evaluation of the material will be done on an ongoing basis and will be based on the following criteria:
      1. appearance and condition
      2. content (currency, accuracy, etc)
      3. inappropriate for the collection
      4. age of materials
   B. Materials that are not to be discarded but can be replaced due to poor condition will include:
      1. literature classics
      2. local and state history

VI. **Policies and Procedures for Handling Challenged Materials**
   Any teacher, administrator, student, or PVYSC staff may register a complaint using the following procedure:
   A. The initial complaint shall be made directly to the media specialist either verbally or in writing. Every effort will be made to handle concerns and complaints at this level. If the issue cannot be resolved at this level, a written complaint may be filed with the school administrator.
   B. If filing a written complaint, District 6's *Public Concerns/Complaints About Instructional Resources* policy shall be used (see appendix E)
   C. A committee made up of the school administrator, a language arts teacher, and a facility director will review the materials and make a recommendation within two weeks of the receipt of the written complaint. The written complaint and the recommendation will then be forwarded to the District Six School Board.
   D. The final decision will be based on this committee and the media specialist's joint decision.
   E. The final decision will be put in writing for the committee, School Board, and complainant.
   F. Appeals will be handled by the school administrator and director of the facility, who will make the final decision jointly.

VII. **Copyright Policy**
   The PVYSC library will comply with School District 6's copyright policy which supports the United States Copyright Act (see appendix F).

_____

School Administrator

_____

PVYSC Administrator

_____

PVYSC Library Media Specialist

Appendix B

Resources

ADVOCACY

American Correctional Association. Oldest and largest correctional association in the world. Standards and accreditation for correctional facilities. Alexandria, VA: ACA. http://www.aca.org/

Association of Specialized and Cooperative Library Agencies (ASCLA). Division of the American Library Association. Networking, enrichment, and educational opportunities for librarians serving special populations. http://www.ala.org/ala/mgrps/divs/ascla/ascla.cfm

Building Blocks for Youth—Center for Children's Law and Policy. Initiative to address disproportionate minority contact in the juvenile justice system. Washington, DC: Center for Children's Law and Policy. http://www.cclp.org/building_blocks.p

Campaign for Youth Justice. Dedicated to ending the practice of trying, sentencing, and incarcerating youth under the age of 18 in the adult criminal justice system. Washington, DC: Campaign for Youth Justice. http://www.campaignforyouthjustice.org/

Center for Young Women's Development. Supports incarcerated and previously incarcerated young women by helping them develop skills and coping mechanisms needed to successfully reenter the community. San Francisco, CA: Center for Young Women's Development. http://www.cywd.org/gdap.html

Correctional Education Association. Professional association serving educators and administrators to students in correctional settings. Affiliate of the American Correctional Association. Elkridge, MD: Correctional Education Association. http://www.ceanational.org/index2.htm

Council of Juvenile Correctional Administrators. Concerned with juvenile justice policy; provides technical assistance and grants to correctional facilities. Braintree, MA: Council of Juvenile Correctional Administrators. http://cjca.net/

Family & Corrections Network. Information, training, and technical assistance for children and families of prisoners. Jenkintown, PA: Family & Corrections Network. http://www.fcnetwork.org/main.html

Juvenile Justice Project of Louisiana. Advocacy organization focused on transforming the troubled juvenile justice system in Louisiana. New Orleans: Juvenile Justice Project of Louisiana. http://jjpl.org/new/

Library Services to Prisoners Forum. Concerned with the library and information needs of prisoners. http://www.ala.org/ala/mgrps/divs/ascla/asclaourassoc/asclasections/lssps/lspf/lspf.cfm

Literacy for Incarcerated Teens. Working to end illiteracy among New York City's incarcerated youth. New York: Literacy for Incarcerated Teens. http://www.literacyforincarcerated teens.org

National Center on Education, Disability, and Juvenile Justice. Examines the overrepresentation of youth with disabilities at risk for contact with the courts or already involved in the juvenile delinquency system. Has technical assistance, research, and resources. College Park: University of Maryland. http://www.edjj.org/

National Partnership for Juvenile Services. Advocates for the highest standards in care, management, and programming for detained youth; training and professional development opportunities for practitioners; and leading reform efforts. Partners include the National Association for Juvenile Correctional Agencies, the National Juvenile Detention Association, the Juvenile Justice Trainers Association, and the Council for Educators of At-Risk and Delinquent Youth. Lexington, KY: National Partnership for Juvenile Services. http://npjs.org/

Prisoner's Right to Read—Intellectual Freedom Manual, 8th ed. An interpretation of the Library Bill of Rights. Chicago: American Library Association. http://www.ifmanual.org/prisoners

Young Adult Library Services Association (YALSA). Division of the American Library Association. Supports library services to teens. http://www.ala.org/ala/mgrps/divs/yalsa/yalsa.cfm

COLLECTION DEVELOPMENT

Children's Book Committee—Bank Street College of Education. Book lists and reviews; includes teen and young adult literature. New York: Bank Street College of Education. http://www.bnkst.edu/bookcom/

Embracing the Child. Literature for learning and shared reading; investing in the whole child. Includes sections for young adults. http://www.embracingthechild.org/

Extending Library Services to Empower Youth (ELSEY). Information on building meaningful libraries for youth in detention centers. http://elseyjdc.wordpress.com/

GreenBeanTeenQueen. Book reviews, booklists, and musings from a young adult (YA) librarian. http://www.greenbeanteenqueen.com/

Living Justice Press. A nonprofit publisher for restorative justice. Publishes and promotes alternative works about social justice and community healing. St. Paul, MN: Living Justice Press. http://www.livingjusticepress.org/

Street Fiction: Author interviews, news, and reviews of urban books. Created by Daniel Marcou. http://www.streetfiction.org/

YALSA Book Awards & Booklists. http://www.ala.org/ala/mgrps/divs/yalsa/booklistsawards/booklistsbook.cfm

Youthlight, Inc. Educational materials for counselors, educators, mental health professionals, and parents. Chapin, SC: Youthlight, Inc. http://www.youthlight.com/

DIRECTORIES

Directory of State Prison Librarians. State-by-state listings; contains some links to juvenile detention libraries. Baltimore: Maryland Correctional Education Libraries, Division of Workforce Development and Adult Learning. http://www.dllr.state.md.us/ce/lib/celibdirstate.shtml

State Correctional Education Coordinators—U.S. Department of Education. List of coordinators who provide services to inmates who participate in education activities. Washington, DC: U.S. Department of Education. http://wdcrobcolp01.ed.gov/Programs/EROD/org_list.cfm?category_ID=SCE

JUVENILE JUSTICE

Balanced and Restorative Juvenile Justice—Clark County, Washington, Juvenile Court. Website with information on balanced and restorative justice principles. Vancouver, WA: Clark County Juvenile Court. http://www.clark.wa.gov/juvenile/balanced.html#Development

Census of Juveniles in Residential Placement Databook. Characteristics of juvenile offenders in residential placement facilities in the United States. Washington, DC: Office of Juvenile Justice and Delinquency Prevention, U.S. Department of Justice. http://www.ojjdp.gov/ojstatbb/cjrp/

Juvenile Corrections Resources. Website of resources supporting juvenile corrections reform. New York: Andrew Vachss. http://www.vachss.com/help_text/juvenile_corrections.html

Juvenile Info Network—The Corrections Connection Network—Corrections.com. Collection of links to organizations related to juvenile delinquency. Encourages communication among juvenile justice professionals; fosters reform programs. http://www.juvenilenet.org/

Juvenile Justice System Structure and Process—Case Flow Diagram. Describes the stages of delinquency case processing in the juvenile justice system. Washington, DC: Office of Juvenile Justice and Delinquency Prevention, U.S. Department of Justice. http://www.ojjdp.gov/ojstatbb/structure_process/case.html

Kirsten Anderberg's MacLaren Hall History Site. History of a child protection institution in Los Angeles County by a former ward. Ventura, CA: Kirsten Anderberg. http://users.resist.ca/~kirstena/machallto1970.html

National Criminal Justice Reference Service—Juvenile Justice. Justice and substance abuse information supporting research, policy, and program development; over 205,000 publications, reports, articles, and audiovisual products. Washington, DC: Office of Justice Programs, U.S. Department of Justice. http://www.ncjrs.gov/App/Topics/Topic.aspx?TopicID=122

National Institute of Corrections—Library. Online library of unpublished, operationally oriented materials developed by correctional agencies. http://nicic.gov/Features/Library/

National Juvenile Justice Education Data Clearinghouse. Addresses the lack of research and information on juvenile justice education. Tallahassee: Florida State University College of Criminology and Criminal Justice. http://www.criminologycenter.fsu.edu/p/ndc-about-data-clearinghouse.php

National Survey of Youth in Custody. Data on prevalence of sexual assault in juvenile facilities. Washington, DC: Bureau of Justice Statistics, U.S. Department of Justice. http://bjs.ojp.usdoj.gov/index.cfm?ty=dcdetail&iid=321

New York House of Refuge: A Brief History. New York State archives. History of the first juve-
    nile reformatory in the United States. Albany: New York State Department of Education.
    http://www.nysarchivestrust.org/a/research/res_topics_ed_reform_history.shtml
Office of Juvenile Justice and Delinquency Prevention, U.S. Department of Justice. Leadership,
    coordination, and resources to prevent and respond to juvenile delinquency and victimiza-
    tion. Collects statistics on juvenile corrections. http://www.ojjdp.gov/
Survey of Youth in Residential Placement. Information gathered from youth in residential facili-
    ties. Washington, DC: Office of Juvenile Justice and Delinquency Prevention. https://
    syrp.org/default.asp

PROGRAMS FOR YOUTH

Changing Lives through Literature: An alternative sentencing program. Is based on the power of
    literature to transform lives through reading and group discussion. North Dartmouth: Uni-
    versity of Massachusetts. http://cltl.umassd.edu/home-flash.cfm
Cyber High. Electronic high school available via the Internet. Is aligned to California content
    standards, accredited through the Fresno Unified School District, and sponsored by
    Roosevelt High School in Fresno. Fresno, CA: Cyber High. http://www.cyberhigh.org/
Distribution to Underserved Communities Library Program. Distributes books on contemporary
    art and culture free of charge to rural and inner-city libraries, schools, and alternative
    reading centers nationwide. New York: Art Resources Transfer, Inc. http://www
    .ducprogram.org/
Diverse-City. Literary magazine by incarcerated teens. Diverse-City is part of the Hennepin
    County (Minnesota) Library's award-winning Great Transitions program at the Hennepin
    County Home School. http://www.hclib.org/teens/Diverse_City.cfm
Free Minds Book Club & Writing Workshop. Uses books and creative writing to empower young
    inmates to transform their lives. Washington, DC: Free Minds Book Club & Writing
    Workshop. http://www.freemindsbookclub.org/
Free Write: Jail Arts & Literacy. Nancy B. Jefferson School, Cook County Juvenile Detention
    Center. Facilitates creative writing and arts education. Chicago: Free Write: Jail Arts &
    Literacy. http://www.freewritejailarts.org/
Going beyond the Bars: Provides library service to incarcerated youth. Promotes ready
    reference materials to public librarians interested in establishing different types of
    outreach programs to this important social demographic. Created by students Sean
    Eads and Melissa Henderson for the University of Illinois Graduate School of Library
    and Information Science. http://ccb.lis.illinois.edu/Projects/youth/breakfree/definition
    .htm
Great Stories Club. Reading and discussion program targeting underserved, troubled teens.
    Chicago: American Library Association. http://www.ala.org/ala/aboutala/offices/ppo/
    programming/greatstories/club.cfm
InsideOUT Writers. Weekly writing classes within the Los Angeles County Juvenile Hall
    System. Los Angeles: InsideOUT Writers. http://www.insideoutwriters.org/
Libraries, Literacy, and Juvenile Correctional Facilities. A resource overview of libraries in juvenile
    correctional facilities created for a library science course. http://jdclib.wordpress.com/
Maryland Juvenile Services Education Program. Education for incarcerated juveniles in
    Maryland. http://www.marylandpublicschools.org/MSDE/divisions/careertech/juvenile
    _services

National Reentry Resource Center—Library. Library of reentry resources and publications available online. Council of State Governments Justice Center Project. http://www.national reentryresourcecenter.org/library

Nidorf Collective @ UCLA. Student volunteers at the Barry J. Nidorf Juvenile Detention Center in Sylmar, California. Los Angeles: Nidorf Collective, Graduate School of Education and Information Studies, University of California. http://www.studentgroups.ucla.edu/nidorfcollective/

Platte Valley Youth Service Center Library. Helping incarcerated youth in northern Colorado to develop their reading, writing, and thinking skills, and to become more comfortable in a library setting so that they can continue good reading habits once they return to the community. Greeley, CO: Platte Valley Youth Services Center. http://pvysc.colibraries.org/

Prevention and Intervention Programs for Children and Youths Who Are Neglected, Delinquent, or at Risk, U.S. Department of Education. Formula grants to state education agencies for supplementary education services for juveniles in state institutions. Washington, DC: U.S. Department of Education. http://www2.ed.gov/programs/titleipartd/index.html

Prison Libraries—Colorado State Library Institutional Library Development Unit. Includes services to the Division of Youth Services. Denver: Colorado Department of Education. http://www.cde.state.co.us/cdelib/prisonlibraries/index.htm

Reclaiming Futures: Communities help teens overcome drugs, alcohol, and crime. Six-step model involves juvenile courts, probation, treatment, and community. Portland, OR: Portland State University. http://www.reclaimingfutures.org/

Reentry Programs Database—Reentry Policy Council. Descriptions of reentry programs and initiatives across the country in a searchable database. Council of State Governments Justice Center Project. http://reentrypolicy.org/reentry-program-examples/reentry-programs-start

Second Chance Books—Austin Public Library. Gardner Betts Juvenile Justice Center Outreach Program. Austin, TX: Austin Public Library. http://www.ci.austin.tx.us/library/2ndchance.htm

State of Maryland Division of Correction—Education and Vocational Services: Library Services. Policy and procedures for the operation of the Maryland State Department of Education (MSDE) Libraries in the Division of Correction. http://www.dllr.state.md.us/ce/lib/celibmatvocserv.shtml

The Beat Within. Weekly literary magazine by youth in juvenile detention centers. A program of Pacific News Service. San Francisco, CA: The Beat Within. http://www.thebeatwithin.org/news/

Youth Communication: True Stories by Teens. Helps teens develop their reading and writing skills so they can acquire the information they need to make thoughtful choices about their lives. New York: Youth Communication. http://www.youthcomm.org/index.html

BEHAVIOR AND OTHER TEEN ISSUES

Atkin, S. Beth. 1996. *Voices from the Streets: Young Former Gang Members Tell Their Stories.* Boston: Little, Brown.

Community Intervention: Tools to Help Youth. Training seminars on issues related to teens in grades 9–12. Minneapolis, MN: Community Intervention. http://www.community intervention.org/

Desetta, Al. 1996. *The Heart Knows Something Different: Teenage Voices from the Foster Care System.* New York: Persea Books.

Desetta, Al, and Sybil Wolin, eds. 2000. *The Struggle to Be Strong: True Stories about Teens Overcoming Tough Times*. Minneapolis, MN: Free Spirit.

DiConsiglio, John. 2008. *Out of Control: How to Handle Anger—Yours and Everyone Else's*. New York: Franklin Watts.

Foster, Chad. 1995. *Teenagers Preparing for the Real World*. Duluth, GA: Rising Books.

Fry, Eva. 2005. *Letters from Juvenile Hall: Kids Helping Kids*. Bloomington, IN: AuthorHouse.

Gibbs, John C., Granville Bud Potter, and Arnold P. Goldstein. 2008. The Equip Program: Teaching youth to think and act responsibly through a peer-helping approach. *Reclaiming Children & Youth* 17 (2): 35–38.

Goldstein, Arnold P., Rune Nensen, Bengt Daleflod, and Mikael Kalt. 2004. *New Perspectives on Aggression Replacement Training: Practice, Research, and Application*. Hoboken, NJ: Wiley & Sons.

Humes, Edward. 1996. *NO MATTER HOW LOUD I SHOUT: A Year in the Life of Juvenile Court*. New York: Simon & Schuster.

Lehman, James. *The Total Transformation Program: Behavior Program for Parents of Troubled Teens*. Westbrook, ME: Legacy Publishing. http://www.thetotaltransformation.com

Lelsie, Katharine. 2004. *When a Stranger Calls You Mom: A Child Development and Relationship Perspective on Why Abused and Neglected Children Think, Feel and Act the Way They Do*. Pittsboro, NC: Brand New Day Publishing.

Maultsby, Maxie. 1974. *You and Your Emotions*. Lexington, KY: Rational Self-Help Books.

Maultsby, Maxie. 1984. *Rational Behavior Therapy*. Englewood Cliffs, NJ: Prentice-Hall.

McKay, Matthew, Peter Rogers, and Judith McKay. 1989. *When Anger Hurts: Quieting the Storm Within*. Oakland, CA: New Harbinger Publications.

Munsey, Brenda. 1998. *Moral Development, Moral Education, and Kohlberg: Basic Issues in Philosophy, Psychology, Religion, and Education*. Birmingham, AL: Religious Education Press.

Pranis, Kay. 1998. *Engaging the Community in Restorative Justice*. Washington, DC: U.S. Department of Justice.

Roush, David. 1984. Rational-emotive therapy and youth: Some new techniques for counselors. *Personal & Guidance Journal* 62 (7): 414–417.

Youth Communication. 1998. *Things Get Hectic: Teens Write about the Violence That Surrounds Them*. New York: Simon & Schuster.

References

Agosto, Denise. 2007. Why do teens use libraries? Results of a public library use survey. *Public Libraries* 46 (3):55–62.

Alessio, Amy, ed. 2008. *Excellence in library service to young adults*. 5th ed. Chicago: American Library Association.

Alford, D. J., and K. A. Larson. 1987. Cognitive problem solving: An effective model for implementing a comprehensive training program in a correctional setting. *Journal of Correctional Education* 38 (2):71–76.

American Correctional Association. 2003. *National juvenile detention directory.* Lanham, MD: American Correctional Association.

American LIbrary Association. 1942. *Basic book collection for high schools.* Chicago: American Library Association.

Angier, Naomi. 2003. Juvenile Justice Outreach Library Program. *OLA Quarterly* 9 (3):15.

Angier, Naomi, Rebecca Cohen, and Jill Morrison. 2001. Juvenile justice outreach: Library services at detention centers. *PNLA Quarterly* 66 (1):16.

Angier, Naomi, and Katie O'Dell. 2000. The book group behind bars. *Voice of Youth Advocates* 23 (5):331–3.

Appel, Rhoda Sara. 1945. Functional library serving boys. *Library Journal* 70:800–2.

Asbury, George B. 1907. Book selection at the Indiana reformatory library. *Library Occurrent* 1 (9):1–2.

Association of Specialized and Cooperative Library Agencies, and American Library Association. 1999. *Library standards for juvenile correctional facilities.* Chicago: American Library Association.

Bardach, E. 2001. Developmental dynamics: Interagency collaboration as an emergent phenomenon. *Journal of Public Administration Research and Theory* 11 (2):149–64.

Benner, Patricia. 1982. *From novice to expert: Excellence and power in clinical nursing practice.* Menlo Park: Addison-Wesley.

Bennion, Lynne Ann. 1986. Consequential thinking in first-time juvenile offenders: A cognitive-behavioral treatment program [doctoral dissertation]. West Lafayette, IN: Purdue University

Berns, C. 2004. Bibliotherapy: Using books to help bereaved children. *Omega* 48:321–36.

Blinn, Cynthia. 1995. Teaching cognitive skills to effect behavioral change through a writing program. *Journal of Correctional Education* 46 (4):146–54.

Bodart, Joni Richards. 2008. It's all about the kids: Presenting options and opening doors. *Young Adult Library Services* 7 (1):35–45.

Branch, O. 1935. Modernizing an old institution's library. *Library Journal* 60:796–7.

Brown, Eleanor Francis. 1975. *Bibliotherapy and its widening applications*. Metuchen, NJ: Scarecrow Press.

Carey, Miriam E. 1907a. Libraries in state institutions. *Bulletin of the American Library Association* 1:101–8.

Carey, Miriam E. 1907b. Libraries in state institutions. *Minnesota Library Notes and News* 2: 67–70.

Carlson, Linda. 1997. A day in detention. *ALKI* 13 (3):18.

Chapman, Mariana W. 1894. Prison reform in its present aspect. *Friends intelligencer* (October 20): 665.

Cheney, Amy. 2009. Re: "Bad words in juvie library" [email communication], February 4, 2009.

Children's Bureau, U.S. Department of Health, Education, and Welfare. 1957. *Institutions serving delinquent children: Guides and goals*. Washington, DC: U.S. Department of Health, Education, and Welfare, in cooperation with the National Association of Training Schools and Juvenile Agencies.

Ciment, James, ed. 2006. *Social issues in America: An encyclopedia*. Armonk, NY: M. E. Sharpe.

Clark County (WA) Juvenile Court. *Balanced and restorative juvenile justice* 2008 [cited March 4, 2010]. Available from http://www.clark.wa.gov/juvenile/balanced.html.

Confessore, Nicholas. 2009. New York finds extreme crisis in youth prisons. *New York Times*, December 14.

Cook, Elizabeth. 1953. Library at the state training school for girls, Geneva, Illinois. *Illinois Libraries* 35:146–8.

Cook, Sherry, R. Stephen Parker, and Charles Pettijohn. 2005. The public library: An early teen's perspective. *Public Libraries* 44 (3):157–61.

Correctional Education Association. 2004. *Performance standards for correctional education programs in juvenile institutions*. Elkridge, MD: Correctional Education Association.

Council of Juvenile Correctional Administrators. 2010. *Performance-based standards: Goals, standards, outcome measures, expected practices and processes*. Washington, DC: CJCA.

Coyle, William J. 1987. *Libraries in prisons: A blending of institutions, new directions in information management*. New York: Greenwood Press.

Darlington, Yvonne, Judith Feeney, and Kylie Rixon. 2005. Interagency collaboration between child protection and mental health services: Practices, attitudes and barriers. *Child Abuse and Neglect* 29:1085–98.

Davis, Veronica A. 2000. Breaking out of the box: Reinventing a juvenile-center library. *American Libraries* 31 (10):58–61.

Disher, Wayne. 2007. *Crash course in collection development*. Westport, CT: Libraries Unlimited.

Dittman, Katherine. 2007. Between the lines: Girls in detention escape into books. *The Monthly* 37 (7).

Dohrn, Bernardine. 2002. The school, the child, and the court. In *A century of juvenile justice*, edited by M. K. Rosenheim, F. E. Zimring, and D. S. Tanenhaus. Chicago: University of Chicago Press.

Doll, Beth, and Carol Doll. 1997. *Bibliotherapy with young people*. Englewood, CO: Libraries Unlimited.

Feldstein, Sarah W., and Joel I. D. Ginsburg. 2009. Sex, drugs, and rock 'n' rolling with resistance: Motivational interviewing in juvenile justice settings. In *Handbook of forensic mental health with victims and offenders: Assessment, treatment, and research*, edited by D. W. Springer and A. R. Roberts. New York: Springer.

Fenster-Sparber, Jessica. 2008. New York City's most troubled youth: Getting caught reading at Passages Academy Libraries. *Knowledge Quest* 37 (1):30–3.

Foster-Fishman, P. G., D. A. Salem, N. A. Allen, and K. Fahrback. 2001. Facilitating interorganizational collaboration: The contributions of interorganizational alliances. *American Journal of Community Psychology* 29 (6):875–905.

Freivalds, Peter. 1996. Balanced and Restorative Justice Project (BARJ). *Office of Juvenile Justice and Delinquency Prevention Fact Sheet* 42 (July).

Ganter, J. 2000. Capture the power of reading. *Illinois Libraries* 82 (3):176–80.

Gilman, Isaac. 2008. Beyond books: Restorative librarianship in juvenile detention centers. *Public Libraries* 47 (1):59–66.

Green, Beth L., Anna Rockhill, and Scott Burns. 2008. The role of interagency collaboration for substance-abusing families involved with child welfare. *Child Welfare* 87 (1):29–61.

Griffin, P. 2003. *Trying and sentencing juveniles as adults: An analysis of state transfer and blended sentencing laws*. Pittsburgh, PA: National Center for Juvenile Justice.

Griffin, P. and Patricia Torbet. 2002. Desktop guide to good juvenile probation practices. Pittsburgh, PA: National Center for Juvenile Justice.

Guerra, Nancy G., Tia E. Kim, and Paul Boxer. 2008. What works: Best practices with juvenile offenders. In *Treating the juvenile offender*, edited by R. D. Hoge, N. G. Guerra, and P. Boxer. New York: Guilford Press.

Gunawardena, Sidath, Rosina Weber, and Denise E. Agosto. 2010. Finding that special someone: Interdisciplinary collaboration in an academic context. *Journal of Education for Library and Information Science* 51 (4):210–21.

Harlin, Kasey. 2011. Positive youth development: Achieving Recovery Through Creativity (A.R.T.C.). *Reclaiming Futures*. http://pfh.org/artc/index.php

Hodges, Jane, Nancy Giuliotti, and F. M. Porpotage. 1994. *Improving literacy skills of juvenile detainees*. Juvenile Justice Bulletin. Washington, DC: U.S. Department of Justice Office of Juvenile Justice and Delinquency Prevention.

Hughes-Hassell, Sandra, and Denise Agosto. 2006. Planning library services for inner-city teens: Implications from research. *Public Libraries* 45 (6):57–63.

Ishizuka, Kathy. 2003. NY library gives teens a second chance. *School Library Journal* 49 (11):24.

Jones, Patrick. 2004. Reaching out to young adults in jail. *Young Adult Library Services* 3 (1):16–19.

Jones, Patrick. 2007. Connecting young adults and libraries in the 21st century. *Australian Public Libraries and Information Services* 20 (2):48–54.

Jones, Patrick, Michele Gorman, and Tricia Suellentrop. 2004. *Connecting young adults and libraries: A how-to-do-it manual*. New York: Neal-Schuman Publishers.

Kircher, C. J. 1945. Character formation through books; A bibliography. 2nd edition. Washington, DC: Catholic University of America.

Knepel, Nancy Pokorny, and N. P. Knepel. 1979. Mix skills with fun in a juvenile correctional institution library. *Wisconsin Library Bulletin* 75:57–8.

Krashen, Stephen D. 2004. *The power of reading: Insights from the research.* 2nd ed. Westport, CT: Libraries Unlimited.

Krezmien, Michael P., and Candace A. Mulcahy. 2008. Literacy and delinquency: Current status of reading interventions with detained and incarcerated youth. *Reading & Writing Quarterly* 24 (2):219–38.

Landsberg, Gerald, and Jo Rees. 2009. Forensic practices and serving dually diagnosed youth involved with the juvenile justice system. In *Handbook of forensic mental health with victims and offenders: Assessment, treatment, and research,* edited by D. W. Springer and A. R. Roberts. New York: Springer Publishing Company.

LeDonne, Marjorie, David Christiano, and Jane Scantlebury. 1974. *Survey of library and information problems in correctional institutions.* Washington, DC: United States Department of Health, Education, and Welfare, Office of Education.

Lehman, Wayne E. K., Bennett W. Fletcher, Harry K. Wexler, and Gerald Melnick. 2009. Organizational factors and collaboration and integration activities in criminal justice and drug abuse treatment agencies. *Drug and Alcohol Dependence* 103 (Supplement 1):S65–S72.

Lerman, Paul. 2002. Twentieth century developments in America's institutional systems for youth in trouble. In *A century of juvenile justice,* edited by M. K. Rosenheim, F. E. Zimring, and D. S. Tanenhaus. Chicago: University of Chicago Press.

Life-Changer. 2006. *Library Journal* 131 (5):18–19.

Linden, R. 2002. A framework for collaborating. *The Public Manager* 31 (2):3–6.

Liptak, Adam. 2009. Defining "cruel and unusual punishment" when the offender is 13. *New York Times,* February 3, 12.

Liptak, Adam. 2010. Justices limit life sentences for juveniles. *New York Times,* May 18.

Lu, Ya Ling. 2005. *How children's librarians help children cope with daily life: An enhanced readers' advisory service* [doctoral dissertation]. Los Angeles: Department of Information Studies, UCLA.

Madenski, Melissa. 2001. Books behind bars. *School Library Journal* 47 (7):40–2.

Maloney, D., D. Romig, and T. Armstrong. 1988. Juvenile probation: The balanced approach. *Juvenile and Family Court Journal* 39 (3):1–63.

May, Margaret M. 1953. Books for disturbed children. *Library Journal* 78:1809–12.

McLellan, Kathy, and Tricia Suellentrop. 2007. Serving teens doing time. *Voice of Youth Advocates* 30 (5):403–7.

Methven, Mildred Louise. 1943. Objectives for institution libraries as developed in Minnesota. *ALA Bulletin* 37:403.

Meyers, Elaine. 1999. The coolness factor: Ten libraries listen to youth. *American Libraries* 30 (10):42–45.

Moore, John E., and J. E. Moore. 1963. Ingredients of the correctional school library. *Association of Hospital and Institution Libraries Quarterly* 3:18–22.

msnbc.com. 2007. Teens' brains hold key to their impulsiveness. Associated Press.

Neighbors, I. A., L. Green-Faust, and K. Van Beyer. 2004. Curricula development in forensic social work at the MSW and post-MSW levels. In *Social work and the law: Proceedings of the National Organization of Forensic Social Work, 2000.* Binghamton, NY: Haworth Press.

New York City Department of Juvenile Justice. 2007. *Youth population overview: Admission to detention.* New York: New York City Department of Juvenile Justice.

New York State Archives. *New York House of Refuge: A brief history.* Albany: New York State Education Department [cited July 1, 2010]. Available from http://www.nysarchive strust.org/a/research/res_topics_ed_reform_history.shtml.

Office of Juvenile Justice and Delinquency Prevention. 1997. *Arts programs for juvenile offenders in detention and corrections.* Washington, DC: U.S. Department of Justice [cited March 25, 2011]. Available from http://www.ojjdp.gov/grants/grantprograms/discr14 .html.

Office of Juvenile Justice and Delinquency Prevention. 2008. *Census of juveniles in residential placement databook.* Washington, DC: US Department of Justice, Office of Justice Programs, Office of Juvenile Justice and Delinquency Prevention.

Office of Juvenile Justice and Delinquency Prevention. 2008. How OJJDP is serving children, families, and communities. Annual Report. Washington, DC: US Department of Justice, Office of Justice Programs, Office of Juvenile Justice and Delinquency Prevention.

Oiye, J. A. 1982. Full time, multi-media service to juvenile hall patrons. *Voice of Youth Advocates* 5:16–18.

Pehrsson, D., and P. McMillen. 2005. A bibliotherapy evaluation tool: Grounding counselors in the therapeutic use of literature. *Arts in Psychotherapy* 32 (1):47–9.

Polivka, Barbara J., Sereana Dresbach, Joe Heimlich, and Michael Elliot. 2001. Interagency relationships among rural early intervention collaboratives. *Public Health Nursing* 18 (5):340–9.

Provan, Keith G., Mark A. Veazie, Nicolette I. Teufel-Shone, and Carol Huddleston. 2004. Network analysis as a tool for assessing and building community capacity for provision of chronic disease services. *Health Promotion Practice* 5 (2):174–81.

Puritz, Patricia, and Mary Ann Scale. 1998. *Beyond the walls: Improving conditions of confinement for youth in custody.* Washington, DC: Office of Juvenile Justice and Delinquency Prevention.

Redding, Richard E. 2010. Juvenile transfer laws: An effective deterrent to delinquency? In *Juvenile Justice Bulletin.* Washington, DC: Office of Juvenile Justice and Delinquency Prevention.

Renwick, Brittney L. 2009. *The expansion of a domestic violence program to provide bibliotherapy services to children.* Long Beach: Department of Social Work, California State University, Long Beach.

Rivard, Jeanne C., and Joseph P. Morrissey. 2003. Factors associated with interagency coordination in a child mental health service system demonstration. *Administration and Policy in Mental Health and Mental Health Services Research* 30 (5):397–415.

Rosenheim, Margaret. 2002. The modern American juvenile court. In *A century of juvenile justice,* edited by M. Rosenheim, F. E. Zimring, and D. S. Tanenhaus. Chicago: University of Chicago Press.

Rosenheim, Margaret K., Franklin E. Zimrung, David S. Tanenhaus, and Bernardine Dohrn, eds. 2002. *A century of juvenile justice.* Chicago: University of Chicago Press.

Ross, R. R., E. Fabiano, and R. Ross. 1988. (Re)habilitation through education: A cognitive model for corrections. *Journal of Correctional Education* 39 (2):44–7.

Rozalski, Michael, Marilyn Deignan, and Suzanne Engel. 2008. The world of juvenile justice according to the numbers. *Reading & Writing Quarterly* 24 (2):143–7.

Secret, Mosi. 2011. States prosecute fewer teenagers in adult courts. *New York Times,* March 5, 1.

Shepherd, Robert E. 2003. Still seeking the promise of *Gault*: Juveniles and the right to counsel. *Criminal Justice* 18 (2):22–7.

Sickmund, Melissa. 2004. *Juveniles in corrections*. Washington, DC: Office of Juvenile Justice and Delinquency Prevention.

Sickmund, Melissa, T. J. Sladky, and Wei Kang. 2008. *Census of juveniles in residential placement databook*. Washington, DC: Office of Juvenile Justice and Delinquency Prevention.

Singer, Jonathan B. 2009. From Augustus to BARJ: The evolving role of social work in juvenile justice. In *Handbook of forensic mental health with victims and offenders: Assessment, treatment, and research*, edited by D. W. Springer and A. D. Roberts. New York: Springer.

Smith, Alice G. 1989. Will the real bibliotherapist please stand up? *Journal of Youth Services in Libraries* 2 (3):241–9.

Snedden, David Samuel. 1907. Administration and educational work of American juvenile reform schools [doctoral dissertation]. New York: Teachers College, Columbia University.

Snelling, William Joseph. 1837. *The rat-trap, or, cogitations of a convict in the house of correction*. Boston: G. N. Thomson, Weeks & Jordan.

Sorensen, Elaine Shaw. 1993. *Children's stress and coping: A family perspective*. New York: Guilford Press.

Springer, David W., and Albert R. Roberts, eds. 2009. *Handbook of forensic mental health with victims and offenders: Assessment, treatment, and research*. New York: Springer.

Sturm, Brian W. 2003. Reader's advisory and bibliotherapy: Helping or healing? *Journal of Educational Media and Library Sciences* 41 (2):171–9.

Sweeney, Jennifer. 2008. Transforming the rational perspective on skill development: The Dreyfus Model in library reference work. *Advances in Library Administration and Organization* 26:1–39.

Tanenhaus, Daniel S. 2002. The evolution of juvenile courts in the early twentieth century: Beyond the myth of immaculate construction. In *A century of juvenile justice*, edited by M. K. Rosenheim, F. E. Zimring, and D. S. Tanenhaus. Chicago: University of Chicago Press.

Travers, John F. 1982. *The growing child*. Glenview, IL: Scott, Foresman & Company.

Veysey, Bonita M. 2008. Mental health, substance abuse, and trauma. In *Treating the juvenile offender*, edited by R. D. Hoge, N. G. Guerra, and P. Boxer. New York: Guilford Press.

Vogel, Amanda, Pamela Ransom, Sidique Wai, and Daria Luisi. 2007. Integrating health and social services for older adults: A case study of interagency collaboration. *Journal of Health and Human Services Administration* 30 (2):199–228.

Vogel, Brenda. 1995. *Down for the count: A prison library handbook*. Metuchen, NJ: Scarecrow Press.

Walter, Virginia, and Elaine Meyers. 2003. *Teens and libraries: Getting it right*. Chicago: American Library Association.

Willison, Janeen Buck, Daniel P. Mears, Tracey Shollenberger, Colleen Owens, and Jeffrey A. Butts. 2010. *Past, present, and future of juvenile justice: Assessing the policy options (APO)*. Washington DC: The Urban Institute.

Zimring, Franklin E. 2002. The common thread: Diversion in the jurisprudence of juvenile courts. In *A century of juvenile justice*, edited by M. K. Rosenheim, F. E. Zimrung, and D. S. Tanenhaus. Chicago: University of Chicago Press.

Index

About the Author

JENNIFER SWEENEY, MSLS, PhD, teaches in the College of Information Science and Technology at Drexel University. Dr. Sweeney was a recipient of the 2010 American Library Association Diversity Research Grant investigating the nature and scope of juvenile detention library services in a national survey. Prior to coming to Drexel, she was a senior researcher in the University of California Davis School of Education, analyst with the University of California Davis Library, reference librarian at American University Library in Washington, DC, and librarian with Cost Engineering Research In Arlington, VA. She earned her MSLS from Catholic University and her PhD from UCLA.

Edwards Brothers, Inc.
Thorofare, NJ USA
December 20, 2011